Climate Change in the European Alps

ADAPTING WINTER TOURISM AND NATURAL HAZARDS MANAGEMENT

Edited by:
Shardul Agrawala

OECD

ORGANISATION FOR ECONOMIC CO-OPERATION AND DEVELOPMENT

ORGANISATION FOR ECONOMIC CO-OPERATION AND DEVELOPMENT

The OECD is a unique forum where the governments of 30 democracies work together to address the economic, social and environmental challenges of globalisation. The OECD is also at the forefront of efforts to understand and to help governments respond to new developments and concerns, such as corporate governance, the information economy and the challenges of an ageing population. The Organisation provides a setting where governments can compare policy experiences, seek answers to common problems, identify good practice and work to co-ordinate domestic and international policies.

The OECD member countries are: Australia, Austria, Belgium, Canada, the Czech Republic, Denmark, Finland, France, Germany, Greece, Hungary, Iceland, Ireland, Italy, Japan, Korea, Luxembourg, Mexico, the Netherlands, New Zealand, Norway, Poland, Portugal, the Slovak Republic, Spain, Sweden, Switzerland, Turkey, the United Kingdom and the United States. The Commission of the European Communities takes part in the work of the OECD.

OECD Publishing disseminates widely the results of the Organisation's statistics gathering and research on economic, social and environmental issues, as well as the conventions, guidelines and standards agreed by its members.

This work is published on the responsibility of the Secretary-General of the OECD. The opinions expressed and arguments employed herein do not necessarily reflect the official views of the Organisation or of the governments of its member countries.

Photo Credits:
Figure 14. Christine Rothenbühler, Academia Engiadina, Samedan, Switzerland.
Figure 15. Markus Weidmann, Chur, Switzerland.
Figure 16. Christine Rothenbühler, Academia Engiadina, Samedan, Switzerland.
Figure 17. Christine Rothenbühler, Academia Engiadina, Samedan, Switzerland.

Foreword

Climate change poses a serious challenge to social and economic development in all countries. Clearly, while there is a need to negotiate international commitments to reduce greenhouse gas emissions, there is also a need to place climate change and its impacts within the mainstream of sectoral and economic policies in both developing and developed countries.

It is within this context that the OECD has undertaken work on adaptation to climate change since 2002. While the initial focus was on mainstreaming adaptation within development co-operation, more recent work has also focused on developed country contexts. This volume on "Adaptation to Climate Change in the European Alps: Focus on Winter Tourism and Natural Hazards" is an output from this work.

This work was overseen by OECD's Working Party on Global and Structural Policies. Shardul Agrawala edited this volume and managed the project leading up to it. Simone Gigli provided valuable feedback and input throughout the project. Jane Kynaston, Kathleen Mechali, Elizabeth Corbett and Carolyn Sturgeon-Bodineau provided invaluable staff support for the book and the project. In addition to the authors of this volume, contributions from Guillaume Prudent (Pôle Grenoblois d'Étude et de Recherche pour la Prévention des Risques Naturels), Anne-Sophie Robin (École Nationale Supérieure Agronomique de Montpellier) and Jonas Franke (University of Bonn) are also gratefully acknowledged.

This work has further benefited from discussions with or comments from Martin Beniston (University of Geneva), Marc Gilet (ONERC), Max Gretener (ASA/SVV), Thomas Hlatky (Grazer Wechselseitige Versicherung AG/CEA), Andreas Kääb (University of Oslo), Martin Kamber (IRV/UIR), Ellina Levina (OECD), Roberto Loat (FOEN), Helen Mountford (OECD), Roland Nussbaum (MRN/CEA), Elisabeth Ottawa (BMF), Franz Prettenthaler (University of Graz), Magali Pinon-Lecomte (DPPR), Florian Rudolf-Miklau (BMLFUW), Markus Stoffel (University of Geneva), Gerhard Wagner (UNIQA), Christian Wilhelm (Forestry Services, Grisons), and participants at the OECD-Wengen Workshop on Adaptation to Climate Change in the European Alps in October 2006.

Contributors

Bruno Abegg (*University of Zurich*)

Simon Jetté-Nantel (*OECD*)

Florence Crick (*University of Oxford*)

Anne de Montfalcon (*Université de Paris Dauphine*)

Table of Contents

Tables

Figures

Boxes

List of Acronyms

ANPNC	National Association of Artificial Snow Professionals (Association Nationale des Professionnels de la Neige de Culture)
a.s.l.	Above sea level
BMF	Austrian Federal Ministry of Finance (Bundesministerium für Finanzen)
BMLFUW	Austrian Federal Ministry of Agriculture, Forestry, Environment and Water Management (Bundesministerium für Land- und Forstwirtschaft, Umwelt und Wasserwirtschaft)
BWV	Austrian Federal Office of Hydraulic Engineering (Bundeswasserbauverwaltung)
CARIP	Unit for Analysis of Risks and Preventive Information (Cellule d'Analyse des Risques et d'Information Préventive)
CCR	Caisse Centrale de Réassurance
CDD	Diversified Development Contract (Contrat de Développement Diversifié)
CHF	Swiss Francs
CIM	Cantonal Insurance Monopoly
CIPRA	International Commission for the Protection of the Alps (Commission Internationale pour la Protection des Alpes)
CPER	State-Region Planning Contract (Contrat de Plan Etat Region)
DETEC	Swiss Department of Environment, Transport, Energy and Communications
DPPR	Directorate for the Prevention of Pollution and Risks (Direction de la Prévention des Pollutions et des Risques)
EEA	European Environment Agency
EU	European Union
EUR	Euros
FCOP	Swiss Federal Office for Civil Protection
FIS	International Ski Federation (Fédération Internationale de Ski)
FOEN	Swiss Federal Office for the Environment
GCM	General Circulation Model
GLOF	Glacier Lake Outburst Flood
MEDD	French Ministry of Ecology and Sustainable Development (Ministère de l'Écologie et du Développement Durable)
MISILL	French Ministry of the Interior (Ministère de l'Intérieur, de la Sécurité Intérieure et des Libertés Locales)
MRN	Insurer's Mission for Natural Hazards Awareness and Prevention (Mission des sociétés d'assurances pour la Connaissance et la Prévention des risques naturels)

List of Acronyms (continued)

NAO   North Atlantic Oscillation
NGO   Non-Governmental Organisation
PACE   EU Permafrost And Climate in Europe
PERMOS   Permafrost Monitoring Switzerland
PPR   Risks Prevention Plan (Plan de Prévention des Risques naturels)
RCM   Regional Climate Model
WLV   Austrian Federal Torrent and Avalanche Control Authority (Wildbach- und
          Lawinenverbauung)

Executive Summary

This report provides an assessment of the impacts of, and adaptation to, climate change in the areas of winter tourism and natural hazards management for the European Alps.[1] The implications of this assessment however extend beyond the European Alps. Insights into the costs of adaptation, the roles of the private sector and government agencies, and broader lessons on the synergies and trade-offs between climate change adaptation and other sectoral and development priorities are also likely to be relevant for other mountain systems which face similar climatic and contextual challenges, for example in North America, Australia and New Zealand. More generally, examining the case of the European Alps – where there is high adaptive capacity – can highlight examples of good adaptation practices and the role of financial mechanisms, as well as identify constraints and limits to adaptation. Such insights would be valuable not only for other developed country contexts, but for developing countries as well.

Climate change is already affecting the European Alps, and adaptation is of vital importance

The Alps are particularly sensitive to climate change, and recent warming has been roughly three times the global average. The years 1994, 2000, 2002, and particularly 2003 have been the warmest on record in the Alps in the past 500 years. Climate models project even greater changes in the coming decades, including a reduction in snow cover at lower altitudes, receding glaciers and melting permafrost at higher altitudes, and changes in temperature and precipitation extremes. These climatic changes are impacting a system that is not only of critical economic and ecological importance, but one which is also already vulnerable to a wide range of natural hazards as well as demographic and environmental pressures. The viability of measures to adapt to the impacts of climate change is therefore of critical importance for Alpine countries. This has been recognised by the Alpine Convention, which in late 2006 invited member countries to develop adaptation strategies promptly for the most affected sectors. Alongside, a recent Europe-wide assessment has identified increasing losses in winter tourism due to reduced snow cover and the increased exposure of settlements and infrastructure to natural hazards as the primary vulnerabilities to climate change in the Alps. These two sectors are therefore the focus of this in-depth analysis.

---

[1] The Alps include five OECD Members (France, Switzerland, Italy, Austria, and Germany) as well as Monaco, Lichtenstein and Slovenia.

Winter tourism is particularly vulnerable, but sensitivity to climate change varies across the Alpine arc

Under present climate conditions, 609 out of the 666 (or 91%) Alpine ski areas in Austria, France, Germany, Italy, and Switzerland can be considered as naturally snow-reliable. The remaining 9% are already operating under marginal conditions. The number of naturally snow-reliable areas would drop to 500 under 1 °C, to 404 under 2 °C, and to 202 under a 4 °C warming of climate. This is the first systematic cross-country analysis of snow-reliability under climate change for the Alps and covers more than 80% of the skiing domain. While the precise numbers are a function of the assumptions made, it is the overall trend as well as the spatial heterogeneity in the impacts which are of policy relevance. Sensitivity to climate change varies markedly among the Alpine countries. Germany is most sensitive, with only a 1 °C warming leading to a 60% decrease (relative to present) in the number of naturally snow-reliable ski areas. Practically none of the ski areas in Germany will be left naturally snow-reliable under a 4 °C warming. Switzerland, meanwhile, is the least sensitive of the five countries, with a 1 °C warming leading to only a 10% decrease, while a 4 °C warming would lead to a 50% decrease (relative to present) in the number of naturally snow-reliable areas. There will also be "winners" and "losers", both in terms of regions – for example Alpes Maritimes, Styria, and Friuli-Venezia-Giulia are considerably more vulnerable than Grisons, Valais, and Savoie – and in terms of the ski areas themselves, with low-lying ski areas being considerably more vulnerable than areas with high altitudinal range.

The winter tourism industry is already adapting to climate change, but there are costs and limits

The winter tourism industry has responded to the implications of observed changes, and a range of technological and behavioural adaptation measures have been put into practice. Artificial snow-making remains the dominant adaptation strategy. Other measures include grooming of ski slopes, moving ski areas to higher altitudes and glaciers, protecting against glacier melt with white plastic sheets, diversification of tourism revenues, and the use of insurance and weather derivatives. Adaptation measures also have costs, as well as limits. Snow-making has proven cost-effective, but such estimates are based only on the direct financial costs to ski operations and do not include the potential externalities of such practices on water consumption, energy demand, landscape, or ecology. Furthermore, snow-making costs will increase non-linearly as temperatures increase – and if ambient temperatures increase beyond a certain threshold snow-making will simply not be viable. Likewise, grooming of ski slopes can reduce the minimum snow-depth required for ski operations by 10 or 20 cm. However, no amount of grooming can overcome significant declines or the total absence of snow cover. Similarly, plastic sheets have been shown to be cost-effective in protecting glacier mass, but there are limits to the area that can be covered by such sheets and they cannot prevent the eventual disappearance of glaciers if warming trends continue. Insurance, meanwhile, can reduce the financial losses from occasional instances of snow-deficient winters, but cannot protect against systemic long-term trends towards warmer winters.

Governments can also play a key role in facilitating sustainable adaptation in winter tourism

A key issue for governments is the degree of oversight that might be needed in what is, to a large extent, autonomous adaptation driven by market forces. One place where the government role might be critical is with regard to the environmental and social externalities that might be created by the implementation (or over-implementation) of particular adaptation strategies. For example, snow-making has implications on water and energy consumption, the grooming of ski slopes can reduce slope stability, while moving ski operations to higher altitudes can threaten fragile environments. Currently policies vary considerably, both across and within countries. France and Germany do not have regulations regarding snow-making, although some aspects are covered within existing regulations for water withdrawal. Austria, meanwhile, has explicit regulations, but they vary across provinces, while in Italy only South Tyrol has snow-making regulations. In Switzerland, meanwhile, snow cannons are subject to environmental impact assessment and there are specific regulations on where they can be used. Regulations vary similarly – or are absent entirely – for the use of snow additives, grooming of ski slopes, and moving ski activities to higher altitudes.

Yet another place where public policy might play a role is in facilitating transition for those at the "losing" end of the adaptation equation. This is because climate change impacts have significant equity implications. Smaller resorts, which also tend to be at low altitudes are both more vulnerable to climate change and have fewer resources for expensive adaptations. Meanwhile, ski conglomerates have lower climate risk (as their ski areas often have greater altitudinal range), better diversification of risk (as they operate a number of resorts), and more resources to make adaptation. Here again public policies vary considerably, from *laissez faire* (let the market decide) to the provision of financial support to those who are most vulnerable. In particular, a key tension that governments and local communities need to confront jointly is between adaptation measures that tend to protect the *status quo* for as long as possible despite increasingly unfavourable climatic conditions, and those which facilitate a smoother transition to the new realities of the changing climate. Overall, there has been more emphasis on preserving the *status quo*, and less on transitions that might be economically and politically expensive in the short-term.

Implications of climate change on natural hazards in the Alps are complex and hazard-specific

The second case examined in this report – natural hazards – is both linked to, and yet significantly different from, winter tourism. While climate change has clearly discernible impacts on winter tourism, its implications on a diverse array of natural hazards that are already prevalent in the Alps are much more complex. Furthermore, while adaptation in winter tourism has largely been autonomous and initiated primarily by the private sector, any responses to address the implications of climate change on natural hazards will almost certainly involve public agencies, require much more co-ordination and planning, and would be superimposed on existing policies and measures to deal with natural hazards. The necessity of suitable adaptation measures to the effects of climate change on natural hazards depends both on the strength of the linkages between climate change and particular hazards, as well as the overall significance of the hazard itself. This analysis concludes that many hazards which have strong linkages to climate change actually have relatively low/medium economic significance. The clearest impacts of climate change on natural hazards occur in glacial and permafrost zones which may be of limited economic significance from a national perspective, although their implications for local communities may be quite significant. On the other hand, hazards which have considerably higher economic and social significance, such as floods and windstorms, have more complex and less certain linkages with climate change. Despite the uncertainty of climate change impacts on floods and winter storms, the risk related to these changes should be taken seriously given the impacts of such events and the growing vulnerability of Alpine societies to such events due to demographic, land-use and other pressures.

Climate change is one additional reason for effective management of current hazards

How best, then, to take climate change risks into account in dealing with natural hazards in the Alps? Clearly, a multi-pronged approach is needed. A natural place to start would be from the institutional structures and risk transfer mechanisms that already exist in the Alpine countries to deal with natural hazards. Climate change and its implications (even if uncertain) are one more reason to improve the efficiency of such structures and mechanisms. The three Alpine countries (France, Switzerland and Austria) examined in this part of the in-depth analysis clearly have very high adaptive capacities with regard to dealing with natural hazards. Institutional structures and regulations for managing natural hazards are in place, as are insurance mechanisms to facilitate risk transfer. While early hazard mitigation efforts focused primarily on disaster recovery, there has been growing emphasis on integrated natural hazards management that includes all elements of the risk cycle (from prevention to recovery). The Alpine Convention is also fostering the implementation of integrated management of hazards across the Alpine arc. Integrated hazard management offers several obvious entry-points for factoring in climate risk information, for example in hazard mapping, spatial planning, as well as the design of prevention measures. However this assessment also demonstrates that the Alpine countries nevertheless face significant challenges in dealing with current hazards, let alone the implications of climate change. For example, integrated management schemes are not yet fully operational, and in many cases implementation remains difficult. It is also noteworthy that, in all countries surveyed, there appears to be very little use of economic incentives to support and strengthen actual hazard prevention efforts. Insurance premiums, for example, are generally not linked to risk exposure, thereby reducing the incentives for undertaking risk prevention.

Climate change adaptation also requires more flexible and forward-looking natural hazards management

Natural hazards management traditionally relies on retrospective information which will no longer be appropriate if climate change alters hazard profiles and distribution. There is therefore a need for more forward-looking approaches that also consider anticipated climate risks. One strategy might be to raise the precautionary standard for hazards management, as including more intense and extreme events into the planning process will enhance resilience to climate change. For example, in Switzerland hazards maps have been adjusted to include events with a 300 year return period instead of being limited to 100 year events. Adjustments have also been made in the planning of emergency measures which now account for events with a 1 000 year return period. Another strategy would be to update hazard maps more frequently to enable decision-makers to take evolving hazard profiles into account, as is the case for permafrost and glacier hazards. Frequent updating of hazard maps, however, needs to be carefully balanced against the significant costs that this might entail. There might be also high transaction costs, and even legal challenges, if significant changes are made to hazard maps on a frequent basis, particularly if such changes are made purely on the basis of model-based projections. A mid-way solution, however, might be to use hazard maps that incorporate scenarios of future impacts as advisory, and not regulatory, tools.

Much like public decision-makers, insurance companies base their operational practices only on the basis of past hazard events. Going from a pricing methodology based on past evidence to the inclusion of theoretical considerations surrounded by large uncertainties may prove difficult to accept for consumers, and to implement by insurers, especially within a competitive insurance sector. However, awareness of climate change is growing among Alpine insurers. In Austria, private insurers are funding the development of local climate change scenarios while in France a consortium of insurers is examining the consequences of climate change on insurance reserves and pricing. These efforts are still in at an early stage and are yet to translate into changes in operational guidelines.

Active monitoring and risk reduction of climate change related hazards is also needed

Finally, in specific cases where climate related risks are rapidly evolving or the impacts are already evident, as is the case for permafrost and glacial risks, an effective adaptation strategy would be to institute risk monitoring and risk reduction projects. Some progress has been made on both these aspects. The European Union, for example, funded two regional activities: Permafrost and Climate in Europe (PACE) between 1997-2000 and Glaciorisk between 2000-2003, to monitor climate risks. At the project level, meanwhile, there are some examples of infrastructural adaptation measures to the increasing risk of permafrost and glacial hazards under climate change. These include the partial drainage of a potentially dangerous glacial lake on the Monte Rosa on the Swiss-Italian border, and the construction of protective dykes against avalanche and debris flows in Pontresina (Switzerland). While these developments are clearly encouraging, they remain, at best, isolated niche examples relative to the scale of the climatic changes underway in the Alps. There is also a clear need to establish more durable mechanisms for climate hazard monitoring that extend beyond short-term funding cycles, and to ensure that such activities extend beyond research and generate information and tools that can then be used to better incorporate climate risks in hazard maps and natural hazard management policies.

Chapter 1

The European Alps:
Location, Economy and Climate

by
Shardul Agrawala

The Alps are particularly sensitive to climate change and are also of critical economic and ecological importance. They are among the most visited regions, represent the "water tower" of Europe, and are also one of the richest biodiversity hotspots in Europe. This chapter provides an overview of Alpine climate, and highlights the vulnerabilities of the Alpine region to climate change as well as the need for adaptation measures. Recent warming in the Alps has been roughly three times the global average and climate models project even greater changes in the coming decades, including reduction in snow cover at lower altitudes, receding glaciers and melting permafrost at higher altitudes, and changes in temperature and precipitation extremes. In particular, increasing losses in winter tourism due to reduced snow cover and increased exposure of settlements and infrastructure to natural hazards represent primary vulnerabilities to climate change in the Alps. The viability of measures to adapt to the impacts of climate change is therefore of critical importance for Alpine countries. This chapter covers developments in Austria, France, Germany, Italy and Switzerland.

The (European) Alps are a mountain range stretching along an arc of about 1200 kilometres, from Nice to Vienna. They are generally divided into the Western Alps and the Eastern Alps, separated by Rhine and the Splügen pass in eastern Switzerland. The Western Alps are higher, but also shorter and more curved, and are located in France, Monaco, Italy and western Switzerland. The Eastern Alps are longer, and cover eastern Switzerland, Italy, Germany, Liechtenstein, Austria and Slovenia (Figure 1). The Alps are the "water tower" of Europe, source to three principal rivers – the Rhine, Rhône, and the Po. They are also one of the richest biodiversity hotspots in Europe with over 30 000 animal and 13 000 plant species.

Figure 1. **Overview of the Alps**

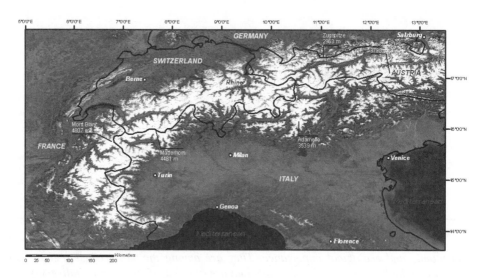

Note: MODIS satellite data distributed by the Land Processes Distributed Active Archive Center (LP DAAC), located at the U.S. Geological Survey (USGS) Center for Earth Resources Observation and Science (EROS) http://LPDAAC.usgs.gov.

The Alpine arc covers an area of about 190 000 square kilometres, and is home to about 15 million people. Most of the population is concentrated in low-lying valleys which are often very densely populated. The Alps are located between two regions of very high population density – the Rhine countries in the north, and northern Italy in the south. Alpine tunnels serve as the most common route for crossing from Northern Europe to the South. The Alps are also among the most visited regions. About 60-80 million people, four to six times the local population, visit the Alps each year as tourists. Meanwhile, mountain agriculture, while closely tied to winter tourism and still very important in this region, has become progressively less economically viable and is increasingly dependent on subsidies.

While contributing to economic development, many of the above trends – the growth and spatial heterogeneity of population and tourism, increased competition between various land-uses, and growth in inter-alpine and trans-alpine transport – have also imposed additional pressures on the environment. In many cases they have increased the vulnerability of the Alpine society to environmental hazards. The implications of climate change on the Alps therefore need to be viewed within this broader socio-economic and environmental context.

1.   Characteristics of Alpine climate

The Alps are bounded by four major climatic influences: the mild, moist air from the Atlantic that flows from the west; the warm Mediterranean air flowing from the south; cold polar air from the north; and the continental air mass (which is cold and dry in the winter and hot in the summer) from the east. The climate in the Alps is also influenced by storms crossing the Atlantic or developing in the Mediterranean. In turn, the Alps themselves also exert considerable influence on weather patterns because of their elevation, vegetation, and snow cover.

The Alps are also characterised by considerable spatial variation in climate, and their physiography plays a key role in determining temperature and rainfall. Valley bottoms are generally warmer and drier than surrounding mountains. Mean January temperatures on the valley floors range from -5 °C to 4 °C, to as high as 8 °C in the mountains bordering the Mediterranean. Mean July temperatures on the valley floors meanwhile range from 15 to 24 °C. Temperature inversions are common during fall and winter up to a height of about 1 000 meters. Temperatures above this altitude are milder than valley bottoms, although at very high altitudes there is again a decline in temperature with altitude. With regard to precipitation, an east-west gradient is observed in the Alps, with less precipitation in eastern Switzerland and Austria than in the western Alps which are exposed to moisture from the Atlantic. In the winter nearly all the precipitation above 1500 metres falls as snow. Snow cover lasts from approximately mid November to the end of May at an altitude of about 2 000 meters. In terms of seasonality, temperatures across the Alps exhibit a peak during the summer months. However, the seasonality of rainfall is much more spatially variable and dependent on location and orography (Frei and Schär, 1998).

2.   Observed climate trends

High resolution reconstructions of the climate in the Alps since 1500 AD show a transition from cold conditions prior to 1900 to the present day warmth during the 20th century and beyond (Figure 2, Casty et al., 2005). The temperature trends have been characterised by increases in winter night-time minimum temperatures by up to 2 °C in the 20th century, and more modest increases in maximum temperatures. The more recent warming observed in the Alps since the mid 1980s, while in step with global warming, is roughly three-times greater than the global average (Beniston, 2005). The most significant warming has occurred since the 1990s. In fact, the years 1994, 2000, 2002, and particularly 2003, have been the warmest on record in the Alps in the past 500 years. Unlike temperature, there is no similar long-term trend in precipitation averaged over the Alps over the past 500 years, although a slight decline in average regional precipitation has been observed since about 1970 (Casty *et al.*, 2005).

The intense warming in the Alps during the 1990s has been linked in part to the behaviour of the North Atlantic Oscillation (NAO). The NAO is characterised by cyclical fluctuations in air pressure and changes in storm tracks across the North Atlantic. The NAO is measured by an index, which is the difference in sea level pressure between a site in Azores (or Portugal) in the mid-Atlantic and another site in Iceland in the North Atlantic. The NAO is believed to particularly influence climate in high elevation regions in the Alps, while low elevation sites in the Alps have much lower sensitivity to it (Beniston, 2000).

Figure 2. **Annual average temperature anomalies in the Alps (relative to 1901-2000 average)**

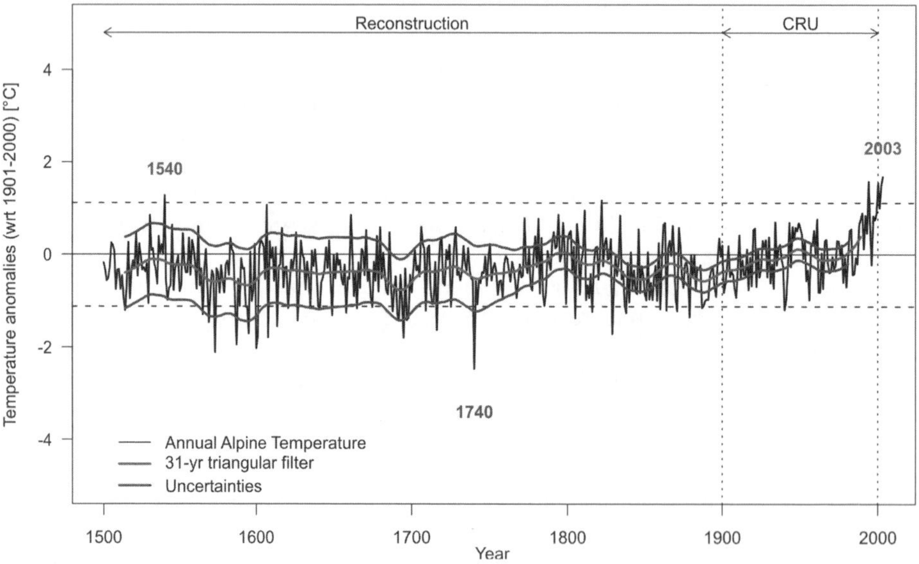

Source: Casty, *et. al.*, 2005. Reproduced with permission granted by John Wiley & Sons Ltd on behalf of Royal Meteorological Society. © Royal Meteorological Society.

The relative attribution of observed climate change in the Alps to global warming or the NAO, however, is not entirely clear. Some recent analyses suggest that a strong positive NAO index since the mid-1980s amplified the warming observed in minimum temperatures in the Alps. In the absence of such NAO forcing, the minimum temperatures in the Alps would not have risen by 1.5 °C during the 20th century, but by 0.5 °C, in line with the global average (Beniston, 2004). The potential influence of the NAO on maximum temperatures meanwhile is not as pronounced. Maximum temperatures would still have risen in the Alps in the latter part of the 20th century (Beniston, 2004).

CLIMATE CHANGE IN THE EUROPEAN ALPS — ISBN 92-64-03168-5 — © OECD 2007

If, however, one examines a much longer historical climate record, the relationship between the NAO and Alpine climate patterns is much more ambiguous. Specifically, it has been shown that the link between a positive NAO index and increase in temperature and/or decline in precipitation in the Alps has only been observed during certain periods in the last 500 years (Casty *et al.,* 2005). Further, the amplification of recent warming is not unique to the Alps but has also been observed at high elevation sites which are not subject to the NAO influence such as the Himalayas (Shreshtha *et al.,* 1998; Liu and Chen, 2002). Finally, it is also not entirely clear whether or not the persistent positive NAO index seen in recent decades (which has been linked to recent changes in Alpine climate) is itself somehow influenced by climate change. The IPCC Third Assessment, for example, notes that "the observed changes in the NAO may well be, at least in part, a response of the system to observed changes in sea surface temperatures" (IPCC, 2001, p.453).

3.   Implications of climate change and key vulnerabilities

General Circulation Models (GCMs) do a very poor job of accounting for the topography of the Alps on account of their coarse spatial resolution and cannot be reliably used on a stand-alone basis to assess future climatic changes and impacts in this region. One approach that is being widely applied is to use GCM outputs as initial and boundary conditions to drive Regional Climate Models (RCMs). RCMs have a resolution of about 20 kilometres (compared to 120 km for GCMs), and can therefore do a better job at incorporating topographic details of the Alps. Although not perfect, such "nested" regional models have done a reasonable job of replicating several aspects of current climate in the Alpine region, which is a prerequisite for their ability to simulate future climatic changes.

Results from such regional climate model simulations for "double-CO_2" indicate a general warming for the Alps in both winter and summer, although summer warming would be more pronounced. Temperatures are also projected to increase much more at higher elevations, which is consistent with observed trends. Further, summer warming in particular is projected to be much more intense over the Western Alps (Heimann and Sept, 2000). Precipitation meanwhile is projected to increase and become more intense over the winter, but be significantly reduced over the summer (Haeberli and Beniston, 1998). These general observations are consistent with climate change scenarios that have been developed for the Swiss Alps, where temperatures are projected to increase by about 1-5 °C in the summer and about 1-3 °C in the winter by 2050, relative to 1990. Precipitation, meanwhile, is projected to increase by about 5-25% in winter, and to decrease by about 5-40% in the summer (OcCC, 2003).

These conditions would result in significant reductions in snow pack and glacier mass within decades. Alpine snow cover shows considerable variation from year to year and over decades. However, recent declines in snow cover in the 1980s and 1990s have been attributed to rising temperatures. The influence of any changes in precipitation on overall snow cover is small and will not affect the overall decline as a result of rising temperatures. From 1850 to 1980 glaciers in the Alps lost approximately 30-40 % of their area and one half of their mass (Haeberli and Beniston, 1998). Since 1980, another 10-20% of the remaining ice has been lost (Haeberli and Hoelzle, 1995). The 2003 hot summer alone led to a loss of 10% of the remaining glacier mass in the Alps. By 2050, about 75% of the glaciers in the Swiss Alps are likely to have disappeared. According to recent research the Alps could lose almost all of their glacier cover by the year 2100 if summer air temperatures increase by 5 °C (Zemp *et al.*, 2006). Climate change is also expected to raise the lower limits of permafrost occurrence by several hundred meters (Hoelze and Haeberli, 1995). Glacier retreat will expose large quantities of moraine sediments and increase slope instability on steeper slopes. Permafrost degradation is likely to contribute to rockfall activity, as was observed in the Matterhorn during the 2003 heatwave (Gruber *et al.*, 2004). Retreat of permafrost also destabilises infrastructure at high altitudes.

Overall, climate change is likely to result in a shifting of hazard zones, which would imply that the use of historical information as a basis for managing hazards will become less relevant (Haeberli and Beniston, 1998). Climate change is also expected to lead to significant changes in the hydrological cycle in the Alps. There is a projected tendency for winter precipitation to fall in more intense events. Furthermore, due to rising temperatures, more of this precipitation is going to fall as rain. Climate change is also going to lead to earlier spring melt and possibly enhance flooding risks in river basins fed by glacier melt. Meanwhile, the projected reduction in summer precipitation is likely to reduce summer season flows in rain-fed basins.

The acute climate change sensitivity of the Alps has been acknowledged by the Alpine Convention in the 2006 Declaration of the IXth Alpine Conference on Climate Change in the Alps. This Declaration emphasises the need for greenhouse gas mitigation efforts by member countries and at the international level. It also calls upon Alpine countries to develop adaptation strategies promptly for the most affected economic sectors including tourism, transportation, agriculture, and forestry, and to address the expected increase in risk related to natural hazards by adopting appropriate risk management measures (Alpine Convention, 2006a).

In its 2005 assessment, the European Environment Agency (EEA) highlighted the following key vulnerabilities for the Alpine region under climate change:

- Increasing risks of economic losses in winter tourism due to warmer winters and less snow cover, especially in low altitudes (*e.g.*, less than 1 500 m).

- Increasing vulnerability of settlements and infrastructure to natural hazards, such as flash floods, avalanches, land-slides, rock fall and mud flows due to heavy rain and snow falls and the upward shift of the snow line.

- Changes in biodiversity and stability of ecosystems, with many Alpine species at risk of being replaced by grassland and trees migrating upland as a result of rising temperatures. Rising temperatures are also increasing the incidence of forest fires.

- Changes in water balance, with water basins with glacier melt being at a greater risk of flooding due to enhanced melting, while basins fed by rainfall might face shortages due to projected declines in summer precipitation.

- Increasing vulnerability of human health and tourism due to heat waves, flash floods and higher pollution from traffic and energy consumption.

4.   Focus of the remainder of this report

The study of adaptation options in this report focuses on the top two vulnerabilities identified in the EEA assessment, namely the increased risk of economic losses in winter tourism due to warmer winters, and the increasing vulnerability of settlements and infrastructure to natural hazards in which climate change could play a contributing role.

Not only are winter tourism and natural hazards management of critical importance to the Alps, they are also activities where the significance of climatic changes is being increasingly felt. In the case of winter tourism the rising snowlines and shorter winter seasons have already resulted in a series of ad-hoc "adaptation" responses by a range of actors, particularly the ski industry. This raises critical issues with regard to the costs and potential externalities of such autonomous adjustments – often by the private sector — as well as their adequacy and limits in the light of future climate change. Meanwhile, in the case of natural hazards and weather extremes, there has been a general trend towards rising losses, although the precise linkages between climate change and any changes in the incidence of such hazards is often unclear. There are also questions of whether and how public agencies, which are engaged in natural hazards management at the national, regional, departmental, cantonal, or local levels, can take climate risks into account. The role of the private sector is also important, particularly through the insurance industry.

These and other related issues are examined in-depth in the following two sections of this report: Chapter 2 focusing on winter tourism, with a particular concentration on France, Switzerland, Austria, Italy, and Germany; and Chapter 3 focusing on natural hazards, with a concentration on France, Switzerland, and Austria.

Chapter 2

Climate change impacts and adaptation in winter tourism

by
Bruno Abegg, Shardul Agrawala, Florence Crick
and Anne de Montfalcon

The winter tourism industry provides a significant contribution to the economy of Alpine countries. This chapter analyses the snow-reliability of the Alpine areas of Austria, France, Germany, Italy and Switzerland, and also provides a comprehensive discussion of adaptation measures and their limits. Under a warmer climate, the number of naturally snow-reliable areas would drop significantly. Sensitivity to climate change varies markedly within the Alpine regions. The winter tourism industry has responded to the implications of observed climatic changes, and a range of technological and behavioural adaptation measures have been put into practice. Artificial snow-making remains the dominant adaptation strategy. However, if warming trends continue, snow-making and other technical measures may not suffice to prevent reductions in snow-reliability. In some regions a transition towards non-snow dependent economic activities might be needed. Governments can play a key role in the adaptation process by overseeing what is, to a large extent, autonomous adaptation driven by market forces, and also by facilitating transition for those at the "losing" end of the adaptation equation. This chapter covers developments in Austria, France, Germany, Italy and Switzerland.

Tourism activities in the Alps generate close to EUR 50 billion in annual turnover and provide 10-12% of the jobs. However, there are disparities between the regions, with tourism activities concentrated in only 10% of the local communities (EEA, 2005). Originally, the main driver of tourism in the Alps was summer tourism. However, with the stagnation of summer tourism since the early 1970s, winter tourism has expanded significantly and compensated for the "crisis of the Alpine summer" (Pechlaner and Tschurtschenthaler, 2003).

There are over 600 ski resorts and 10 000 ski installations in the Alps (WWF Italia, 2006b). The major winter skiing destinations within Europe are the countries of France, Switzerland, Austria and Italy. Those four countries combined provide over 85% of Europe's skiing area[2]. These countries have invested heavily in the skiing industry with the development of a large number of skiing resorts and infrastructure (see Table 1).

Table 1.   **Key numbers in the ski industry in France, Austria, Switzerland and Italy**

Alpine country	Total skiing domain of the country (ha)	% of European skiing domain	Number of ski stations and centres	Number of ski transportation facilities	Turnover of transporation facilities (winter 2003-2004, million Euros	Skier days (winter 2003-2004, million Euros)
France	Over 118 000	30%	308	3865	970	54.8
Austria	79 000	19%	255	3016	901	49.9
Switzerland	84 000	20%	230	1672	588	28
Italy	75 000	18%	200	3100	431	27

Source: Direction du Tourisme, 2004, Direction du Tourisme, 2005, WWF Italia, 2006b.

The winter tourism industry provides a significant contribution to the economy of these countries. For many of the Alpine areas of Switzerland, for example, winter tourism represents the most important source of income and enables the regional economic growth of these rural mountainous areas (König and Abegg, 1997; Bürki *et al.*, 2005). In Austria the winter tourism industry accounts for 4.5% of Austria's GNP and contributes to half of the income made from tourism (Breiling, 1998a; Breiling, 1998b). However, there are large regional and local differences in tourism flows in Austria, with the western Alpine region of Austria contributing the most to the volume of tourism (Breiling, 1998a). The eastern region of Austria experiences a shorter winter season and receives many visitors coming for just one day while the flat northern and eastern areas of Austria do not offer snow-based winter tourism (Breiling and Charamza, 1999). France has the highest winter season turnover amongst all four countries. Within France, the French Alps rank as the number one mountain destination for winter sports. 77.5% of overnight stays related to winter sports and 73.9% of winter sports holidays in France are located in the Alps (Direction du Tourisme, 2004; 2006). Regional differences in winter tourism for the French Alps are detailed in Box 1.

---

[2]   This, however, includes all mountain ranges within these countries.

The Alpine mountain range in France is a prime skiing destination providing tourists with a vast skiing area and well-equipped ski resorts (see Table A).

Table A.   **The importance of ski infrastructure in the French Alps in 2003/2004**

Area (ha)	Number of skiing zones	Number of ski stations / centres	Number of ski lifts	Total area of skiing zones (ha)	Ski runs (estimate) (ha)	Area covered with artificial snow (ha)
Alpes du Nord	147	136	2 186	85 890	16 572	2 339
Alpes du Sud	62	59	721	29 800	4 223	883
Total for the whole Alps	209	195	2 907	115 690	20 795	3 222
% of total for France	64%	64%	75%	84%	83%	80%

Source: Direction du Tourisme, 2002, Direction du Tourisme, 2004.

Within the French Alps the most popular Départements for winter tourism are Savoie, Haute Savoie and the Hautes Alpes. They accounted for 37%, 32% and 14.5% respectively of winter overnight stays in the Alps in 2003/2004 (Direction du Tourisme, 2004), as illustrated in Table B.

Table B.   **Number of winter overnight stays for six departments of the French Alps for the 2003/2004 season**

	Départements of the French Alpes	Number of winter overnight stays in 2003/2004 (in millions)	% of total winter overnight stays in the Alps
Alpes du Nord	Savoie	21.2	37%
	Haute-Savoie	18.1	32%
	Isere	4.7	8%
Alpes du Sud	Hautes Alpes	8.3	14.5%
	Alpes Maritimes	2.5	4.4%
	Alpes de Haute Provence	2.3	4%

Source: Adapted from Direction du Tourisme, 2004.

1.   The impact of climate change on the natural snow-reliability of the Alpine ski areas

The analysis presented in this section covers the Alpine areas of Austria, France, Germany, Italy and Switzerland as defined by the Alpine Convention. In order to assess the impact of climate change on Alpine ski areas, ski resort data, such as altitudinal range and length of ski runs, was collected for more than 750 ski areas across the five countries. However, only ski areas fulfilling specific criteria[3] related to size and type of operation were considered in this analysis[4].

---

[3]   Only medium-size and larger ski areas with at least 3 transport facilities (e.g. ski lifts and chairlifts but not children's lifts) and at least 5km of ski runs were considered. In addition only ski areas with permanent winter operations were taken into account (i.e. weekend- or

Figure 3. **Number of ski areas by country (top) and by region (bottom)**

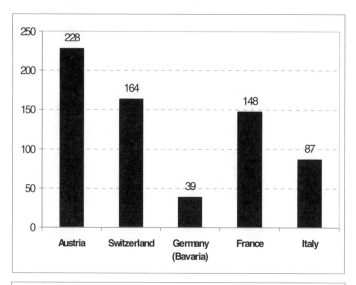

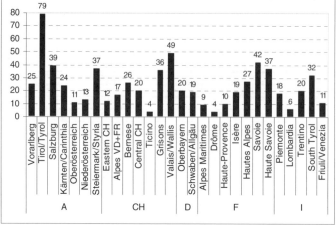

Note: A = Austria; CH = Switzerland; D = Germany; F = France; I = Italy.

These criteria resulted in 666 ski areas being included in this study. The number of ski areas per country and per region is detailed in Figure 3. The classification of the

---

holiday-only ski areas were excluded). Further, ski areas based in the same resort/village but located on opposite sides of the valley (not connected) were regarded as two ski areas. Connected ski areas with separate access and slopes, and/or an individual pricing policy were also counted separately.

[4] For Italy, further information at the level of ski resorts is also available in a background note at www.oecd.org/env/cc/alps

regions adheres in most cases to existing political and administrative boundaries.[5] The mean altitudinal range between the lowest and highest point of the ski areas at a regional level is displayed in Figure 4.

1.1. The 100-day rule and the altitude of natural snow-reliability in Alpine ski areas

In most Alpine ski areas, the operating season covers a period of 120+ days. The season usually starts in the first half of December (some smaller ski areas only begin at the weekend before Christmas) and ends – subject to necessary snow conditions – around Easter/mid-April. The three periods of Christmas/New Year, the February or early spring school holidays and Easter are of crucial importance because of the high demand and high revenues generated in these relatively short time spans. The financial viability of the winter tourism industry depends to a great extent on favourable snow conditions and the snow-reliability of its ski areas. A certain amount of snow is required to groom the slopes, to protect the ground, to guarantee a safe operation, and to offer the skiers an enjoyable experience. The minimum snow depth – from an operational point of view (this may differ from the skiers' perspective) – depends on the nature of the slopes. In general, a snow depth of 30 cm is considered as sufficient, 50 cm as good, and 75 cm as excellent (Witmer, 1986). However, rocky slopes at higher elevations may require a much greater snow depth in order to be skiable (up to 1 m).

Snow cover in the Alps is projected to decrease under climate change, which will, in turn, alter the natural snow-reliability of Alpine areas. In order to investigate the impacts that climate change will have on the winter tourism industry in the Alps it is therefore important to understand the notion of natural snow-reliability. Different criteria have been discussed in order to assess the natural snow-reliability of ski areas (for an overview: see Abegg, 1996). The so-called 100-day rule, first suggested by Witmer (1986), summarises the main points of these studies. It states that in order to successfully operate a ski area, a snow cover sufficient for skiing should last at least 100 days per season. The 100-day rule is not a strict rule, rather a working tool and has been widely accepted among the operators of larger Swiss ski areas (Pfund, 1993, Abegg, 1996).

---

[5]   *Bundesländer* in Austria; *Départements* in France; the *Regierungsbezirke* of Schwaben/Swabia (Allgäu) and Oberbayern/Upper Bavaria in Germany; *Regioni* such as Piemonte and Lombardia in Italy [however, the provinces of Bolzano (Alto Adige/South Tyrol) and Trento (Trentino) were counted separately]; and pre-defined tourism regions in Switzerland, such as Alpes VD + FR (alpine areas of the cantons of Vaud and Fribourg), Valais/Wallis (canton of Valais/Wallis), Bernese Oberland (canton of Bern), Central Switzerland (cantons of Lucerne, Ob-/Nidwalden, Schwyz and Uri), Eastern Switzerland (cantons of Appenzell, Glarus and St. Gallen, and the Principality of Liechtenstein), Grisons (canton of Grisons), and Ticino (canton of Ticino).

Figure 4. **Mean altitude ranges of Alpine ski areas at a regional level**

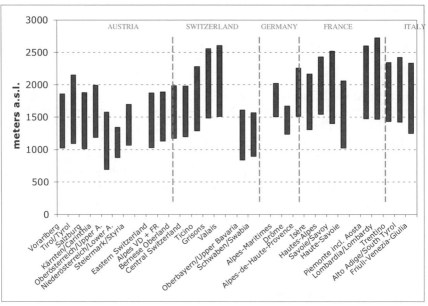

Source: Ski area data for Germany, Switzerland and Italy: DSV-Atlas Ski Winter 2005, ski area brochures (winter 2005/06) and ski area websites. Data for Austria: Bergfex website. Data for France: Ski websites for Alpes de Haute Provence, Alpes Maritimes, la Drôme and l'Isère, and winter tourism brochures for Hautes-Alpes, Savoie and Haute-Savoie.

In Switzerland, Föhn (1990) and Laternser and Schneebeli (2003) found that the criteria for the 100 day-rule (with the 30 cm threshold value of snow depth) are currently fulfilled by areas at an altitude above 1 200-1 300 m above sea level (a.s.l). This suggests that one of the conditions required to run a successful ski business under current climate conditions in Switzerland is a minimum elevation of 1 200 m. This altitude is taken as the line of natural snow-reliability.

The line of natural snow-reliability varies across the Alpine arc, given the considerable variation in Alpine climate. Colder regions will have natural snow-reliability at lower altitudes than warmer regions. Wielke *et al.* (2004), who compared snow cover duration in the Alps, found similar patterns in Switzerland and Austria, except that comparable features are located about 150 m higher in Switzerland than in eastern Austria, indicating a transition from an Atlantic-maritime to a more continental climate. In order to incorporate the effect of continentality (colder winters in the more eastern parts of the Alps), the baseline of natural snow-reliability, as established for Switzerland, has been lowered by 150 m (i.e. 1 050 m for eastern Austria instead of 1 200 m for western Austria and Switzerland). Meanwhile, for Alpine areas influenced by the warmer Mediterranean climate, the snow-reliability line has been raised by 300 m to distinguish them from the northern (cooler Atlantic-maritime

CLIMATE CHANGE IN THE EUROPEAN ALPS — ISBN 92-64-03168-5 — © OECD 2007

climate) parts of the Alps (Witmer, 1986, Matulla *et al.*, 2005; Martin *et al.*, 1994). Consequently, for our study regions the baseline of natural snow-reliability, applying the 100 day-rule, now runs at the new threshold altitudes indicated in Table 2.

Table 2.   **Altitude of the natural snow-reliability line for the Alpine regions of the five countries included in this analysis**

Altitude of natural snow-relia bility line	France	Switzerland	Austria	Italy	Germany
1 050 m			• Salzburg • Steiermark/Styria • Oberösterreich/Upper Austria • Niederösterreich/Lower Austria		• Oberbayern/Upper Bavaria
1 200 m	• Isère • Savoie • Haute Savoie	• Alpes Vaudoises and Fribourgeoises • Valais/Wallis • Bernese Oberland • Central Switzerland • Eastern Switzerland • Grisons	• Vorarlberg • Tyrol • Kärnten/Carinthia (assuming that the 'positive' effect of continentality is offset by the 'negative' effect of the southern latitude)		• Schwaben/Swabia
1 500 m	• Drôme • Hautes Alpes • Alpes de Haute Provence • Alpes Maritimes	Ticino		• Piemonte • Lombardia • Alto Adige/ South Tyrol • Friuli/ Venezia/Giulia • Trentino	

1.2.   Snow-reliability of Alpine ski areas under current and future climate

In a warmer climate, it is estimated that the snowline, as well as the line of natural snow-reliability, will rise by 150 m per 1 °C warming (Föhn, 1990, and Haeberli and Beniston, 1998). On this basis, climate change could result in a 150 m, 300 m and 600 m increase in the altitude of the natural snow-reliability line for 1 °C, 2 °C and 4 °C of warming. This information can now be used to link the concept of natural snow-reliability (100 day-rule) with projected climate change. This results in three different sets of threshold values for present and future conditions:

1.   In regions where the natural line of snow-reliability is currently at 1 050 m, the altitude for snow-reliability will increase to 1 200 m, 1 350 m, and 1 650 m with 1 °C, 2 °C, and 4 °C warming, respectively;

2.   In regions where the natural line of snow-reliability is currently at 1 200 m, the altitude for snow-reliability will increase to 1 350 m (1 °C), 1 500 m (2 °C) and 1 800 m (4 °C).

3. In regions where the natural line of snow-reliability is currently at 1 500 m, the altitude for snow-reliability will rise even higher to 1 650 m (1 °C), 1 800 m (2 °C) and 2 100 m (4 °C).

In this analysis, a particular ski area is considered to be naturally snow-reliable if the upper half of its altitudinal range is located above the threshold value for the line of natural snow-reliability. This assumption is based on the fact that the main ski operations usually take place in the higher parts of the ski areas. Most operators provide "ground-free" access to these higher parts by means of chair-lifts, cable ways etc. in order to guarantee the operation, even if there is a lack of snow at the base of the ski area.

The line of natural snow-reliability is a useful tool to detect trends and patterns in the geographical distribution of naturally snow-reliable ski areas. However, in order to thoroughly analyse a single ski area, additional local factors must be considered in order to account for the complex climatic, topographical and operational reality of each area. For example, Witmer, (1986) provided a detailed analysis of snow depth in relation to aspect and slope: compared with a horizontal surface, depths in late March are twice as great on a 20° north-facing slope, but only 30% of horizontal on a 20° south-facing slope. The results presented below are intended to represent broad patterns and do not account for site specific characteristics.

1.2.1. Results at the national level

Under present climate conditions, 609 out of 666 Alpine ski areas (or 91%) can be considered as naturally snow-reliable (see Table 3 and Appendix 1 for more details). The remaining 9% are already operating under marginal natural conditions. With future climate change the number of naturally snow-reliable ski areas in the Alpine arc could drop to 500 (75% of current Alpine ski areas) with a 1 °C warming, to 404 (61%) with a 2 °C warming and to 202 (30%) with a 4 °C warming of the climate.

Table 3. **Present and future natural snow-reliability of ski areas in the European Alps on a national level**

Country	Number of ski areas	Snow-reliable under current conditions	+1 °C	+2 °C	+4 °C
Austria	228	199	153	115	47
Switzerland	164	159	142	129	78
Germany	39	27	11	5	1
France	148	143	123	96	55
Italy	87	81	71	59	21
Total	666	609	500	404	202

The sensitivity of ski areas to changes in the line of natural snow-reliability differs markedly among the Alpine countries (see Figure 5). Germany is the most sensitive of the Alpine countries considered, with the +1 °C warming scenario leading to a 60% decrease in the number of naturally snow-reliable ski areas. Austria is slightly below average (i.e. slightly more sensitive than the total of all Alpine ski areas), France is about average, and Italy is slightly above average, at least up to an increase of 300 m (plus 2 °C by 2050) in the line of natural snow-reliability. Switzerland is the least sensitive of all five countries, with the percentage of naturally snow-reliable ski areas always above the Alpine average.

Figure 5. **Sensitivity of Alpine ski areas to changes in the line of natural snow-reliability**

(in %, 100= present-day naturally snow-reliable ski areas)

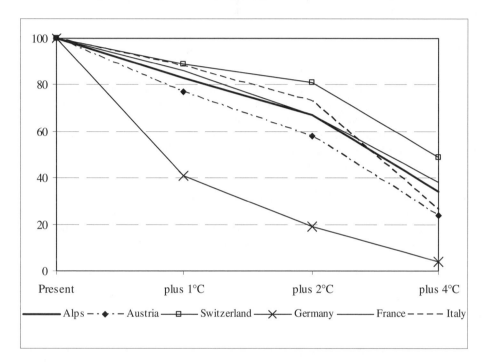

1.2.2. Results at the sub-national (regional) level

A greater insight into the impacts of climate change on winter tourism can be gained by examining the regional results, which are discussed below and presented in Figure 6 and Appendix 1.

Austria

With climate change the natural snow-reliability of the Austrian ski areas will decrease substantially. This is mainly due to the low altitudinal range of the ski areas (see Figure 4). Many of the Austrian ski areas have low base points. For example, the world famous resorts of Schladming and Kitzbühl are situated at only 745 m and 800 m above sea level. The lack of higher altitudes in many of the Austrian mountain ranges makes it impossible to operate on high-elevation sites. The negative effect of the relatively low altitude – for example in comparison to Switzerland – is not offset by the colder, more continental climate in Austria.

With a 300 m rise (plus 2 °C by 2050s) in the line of natural snow-reliability, the number of naturally snow-reliable ski areas in Austria would drop to between 8% (Niederösterreich/Lower Austria) and 62% (Salzburg) of the present level, indicating a strong difference between the most and least sensitive regions in Austria. The north-eastern "Bundesländer" of Lower and Upper Austria will be highly affected, whereas other regions may count on approximately 50% of naturally snow-reliable ski areas.

Switzerland

As mentioned earlier, the Swiss ski areas will be the least affected in the Alps. However, substantial differences exist at the regional level. A vast majority of ski areas in Grisons and Valais/Wallis would remain naturally snow-reliable (83% and 80% respectively), even if the line of natural snow-reliability rose by 600 m (plus 4 °C by 2100). All other regions in Switzerland would be much more affected, with slightly more than 50% of all ski areas being naturally snow-reliable, with a 300 m rise (plus 2 °C by 2050) in the line of natural snow-reliability.

The results presented in this report differ slightly from the results of previous studies on snow-reliability in Switzerland (see Abegg, 1996, and Bürki, 2000). The criteria used in this analysis excluded the low-lying ski areas in the Jura mountain range. In addition, only ski areas with at least three transport facilities and 5 km of ski runs were considered. The changes in the criteria used resulted in a smaller number of ski areas being analysed, most of them situated on higher ground and therefore less prone to changes in the line of natural snow-reliability.

Germany

For Germany, the low-lying ski areas of Bavaria will be highly affected, even by small increases in the line of natural snow-reliability (see Figure 6 and Appendix 1). There is a considerable difference in the percentage of naturally snow-reliable ski areas between Schwaben/Swabia and Oberbayern/Upper Bavaria, with percentages of 47% and 90% respectively under present conditions, and 16% and 40% respectively under the 1 °C warming scenario. According to the regional climate classification for the Alpine arc described by Matulla *et al.* (2005), Swabia belongs to the northwest-southwest climatic region, and Upper Bavaria to the northeast-east climatic region. The difference in the percentage of naturally snow-reliable ski areas can therefore be explained by the different modification of the baseline of natural snow-reliability. However, under a 2 °C warming scenario and a 300 m increase in the line of natural snow-reliability, the percentage of snow-reliable ski areas would drop to 15% for Upper Bavaria and 11% for Swabia, showing hardly any difference between the two sub-regions. In general, the height of the Bavarian Alps offers very little opportunity to operate on higher elevations, making the Bavarian ski areas particularly sensitive to changes in the line of natural snow-reliability.

Figure 6. **Snow-reliability of Alpine ski areas under current conditions and under 1, 2 and 4 °C warming**

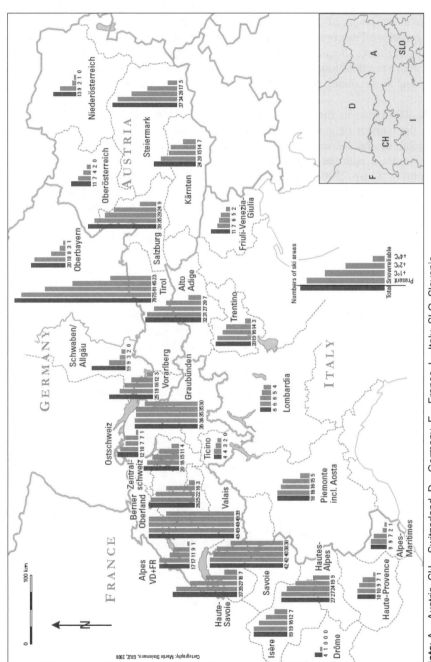

Cartography: Martin Steinmann, GIUZ, 2006

Note: A = Austria, CH = Switzerland, D = Germany, F = France, I = Italy, SLO=Slovenia.

France

In France many ski areas operate at fairly high altitudes (see Figure 4). This is due to the presence of and access to high-elevation mountain ranges (*e.g.*, Mont Blanc) and to the development of "*stations intégrées*" – resorts built for the single purpose of skiing – for which French ski tourism is famous. These resorts, such as Alpes d'Huez, La Plagne, Les Arcs, Tignes and Val Thorens, are usually located at relatively high altitudes above the traditional villages (which are the base for most ski areas in Austria, Germany and Switzerland), and sometimes even above the treeline.

A 300 m rise in the line of natural snow-reliability (+2 °C by 2050) would decrease the number of naturally snow-reliable ski areas to only around 80% of the present total in the Départements of Savoie, Hautes Alpes, and Alpes de Haute Provence (= areas with the highest altitudinal ranges). However, if it were to rise by 600 m (plus 4 °C by 2100), the number of naturally snow-reliable ski areas would decline to 71% for Savoie, 33% for the Hautes Alpes and 10% for the Alpes de Haute Provence. The Départements of the Alpes Maritimes in the South and of Isère and Drôme in the West are more sensitive to changes in the line of natural snow-reliability. The same is true for Haute-Savoie, which has a large number of ski areas operating at lower elevations.

Italy

In general, the Italian ski areas are characterised by high altitudinal ranges (see Figure 4). This is not only due to the access to high Alpine sites, especially in the Northwest, where the highest massifs of the Alps, the Mont Blanc and Monte Rosa, can be found, but also because of the rather high base points of many ski areas. As in France, there are quite a few ski areas starting from high-elevation villages, or from resorts specifically developed for winter sports, with Sestrière being the most famous.

The high altitudes of the ski areas are responsible for a fairly high degree of natural snow-reliability. If the line of natural snow-reliability were to rise by 300 m (plus 2 °C by 2050), the percentage of naturally snow-reliable ski areas in the Italian Alps would drop to 68%. However, there is a gradual decrease in natural snow-reliability from West to East (see Figure 6 and Appendix 1), with the ski areas in Piemonte (in particular the ones in Valle d'Aosta) and Lombardia being the most snow-reliable (83% for both regions), followed by Trentino (70%) and Alto Adige/South Tyrol (63%). In Friuli/Venezia/Giulia, the ski areas are more sensitive, with 45% of them becoming unreliable with a 300 m increase in the line of natural snow-reliability.

2.   Adaptation responses: technological options

Tourism stakeholders and ski operators are not sitting back idly waiting to face the consequences of climate change. They are adapting right now in the expectation of climate change (Burki *et al*, 2005). They realise that the ski industry is highly dependent on snow conditions and that it is at risk from snow-deficient winters. The range of adaptation practices found among ski area operators can be divided into two main categories: technological and behavioural. Technological adaptations appear so far to be the main types of adaptation strategies adopted by tourism stakeholders in the European Alps. There are four main types of technological adaptations: landscaping and slope development; a move to higher altitudes and north facing slopes; glacier skiing; and artificial snow-making.

2.1.   *Landscaping and slope development*

This strategy involves the landscaping of large ski areas (*e.g.*, machine-grading or bulldozing of ski runs, creation of shaded areas) and the contouring or smoothing of smaller areas (*e.g.*, the levelling of rough and bumpy surfaces, and the removal of obstacles such as rocks and shrub vegetation). The aim is to reduce the snow depth required for ski operation, which also enables the reduction of the amount of snow required from artificial snow-making. Additional snow management measures to support this strategy are the erection of snow fences to capture moving snow ("snow farming"), the planting or retention of trees to partially shade the ski runs, and the drainage of wetland areas in order to avoid delayed snow accumulation and premature snow melt. Various strategies are also being used to help prolong snow cover on ski slopes. For example, the use of sheltered ski slopes instead of wind-exposed slopes can help gain 15 days in terms of ski-use, the creation of shaded areas can help gain 30 days and the daily-maintenance and cleaning of ski runs in the winter can help gain 7 days by increasing the snow's albedo (clean snow can have an albedo of up to 90% whereas dirty snow has an albedo of 47%).

In Bavaria, 27% of the skiable domain (999 out of 3 665 hectares) has been modified through landscaping and slope development (Dietmann and Kohler, 2005). 75% of these changes involved machine grading (751 hectares) and 15% was due to forest clearing (152 hectares). These modifications appear to have influenced the area's sensitivity to erosion, as 63% of all damages caused by erosion occurred on modified terrain. As this example demonstrates, the impacts of landscaping and slope development on the Alpine environment need to be considered. Landscaping, in particular bulldozing, has a huge impact on Alpine vegetation. In the process of bulldozing, vegetation and upper soil layers are heavily damaged or even fully removed. Wipf *et al.* (2005), who investigated graded and non-graded plots, found that vegetation responses were highly pronounced on graded ski runs. They found that machine graded ski runs had higher indicator values for nutrients and light, but lower vegetation cover, plant productivity, species diversity, and abundance of early flowering and woody plants. The proportion of bare ground – prone to increased surface runoff and erosion during heavy rain – was almost five times higher on graded than on non-graded plots but was unaffected by re-vegetation measures (sowing) or time since machine grading. Re-vegetation is therefore very difficult to achieve, especially at high altitudes (see also Urbanska, 1997). According to Wipf *et al.* (2005) "machine grading is a particularly damaging management activity, the consequences of which are more severe and long lasting at higher altitudes."

Bulldozing ski runs is also having a negative effect on the attractiveness of the Alpine environment. This may negatively impact summer tourism with hikers unwilling to come to areas that have been altered in such a way. In Switzerland for example, the bulldozing of ski runs is subject to an environmental assessment (Federal Department of Home Affairs, 1991). However, there have been cases of illegal bulldozing, provoking the anger of environmental groups.

2.2. Going higher and facing north

The aim of this strategy is to concentrate ski operations in locations with a climatic advantage. The different options for this strategy include:

- developing north-facing slopes, where the snow pack remains longer;

- moving operations to the upper part of an existing ski area in order to make the best of a given altitudinal range;

- extending an existing ski area to higher elevations including glaciers, where snow cover is generally more reliable and a longer ski season possible;

- building new ski areas at higher elevations including glaciers.

In the last 20 years, many ski lifts (T-bars) have been replaced by chairlifts. The German expression "bodenunabhängige Transportanlagen" (i.e. ground independent transport facilities) describes the advantage of chairlifts over T-bars very well. While T-bars require snow on the ground, chairlifts (and cableways) can provide access to higher areas even when there is no snow on the ground. For example, in situations when there is no snow at the bottom of the station, skiers need to be transported to higher areas where there is enough snow to ski. The replacement of T-bars by chairlifts has, however, also occurred for other reasons linked to higher security standards, higher transport capacity, and greater comfort (in particular for snowboarders).

In 2001, the International Commission for the Protection of the Alps (CIPRA) listed 155 extension projects in the Alps (for Switzerland see also Mathis *et al.*, 2003). Two years later, 12 projects were completed, 26 were approved, 63 were planned, and 54 could still be considered as a future vision. In addition, there were plans to connect existing ski areas (48 projects), and to build new ones in formerly untouched areas (26 projects) (CIPRA, 2003). These projects differ in size, planning status and economic feasibility and therefore in their chances of actually being carried out. Some projects will never be implemented. However, the ideas behind the projects – undertaken or not – are part of a trend towards larger and more snow-reliable ski resorts. An example from Switzerland illustrates the kind of ski area projects that could be initiated in the future. This project, which is not yet approved, is called "Savognin 1900", with the 1900 referring to the altitude. The new resort is planned in a high valley, 11 km from Savognin in the Canton of Grisons. This resort would offer 500 apartments, 1200 hotel beds, and 1500 parking spaces. Furthermore, the existing ski area of Savognin would be extended by one third, including Piz Mez at an altitude of 2 718 m. The estimated costs of this project are CHF 130 million. If this project comes to fruition, this would indicate a radical rejection of the traditional village resort in Switzerland. The key argument used for promoting this project is climate change: "From the hotel straight onto the slopes, that's what guests want, now and in 30 years, when the snowline will have receded due to climate change" (Leutwyler, 2006).

However, this strategy of 'going higher and facing north' faces some constraints:

- Skiers ask for snow-reliability, but they prefer sunny ski runs to shady north-facing slopes.

- For quite a few operators it is an insufficient strategy to successfully cope with changing climatic conditions because of the very limited (and un-extendable) altitudinal ranges of their ski areas.

- Even in cases where it is possible to extend operations to higher altitudes, there might be additional constraints. Climate change scenarios indicate wetter winters, which mean more snow at higher altitudes. While this makes high-elevation ski areas even more snow-reliable, too much snow might actually be the future problem for these areas, as the additional snow will likely lead to an increased risk of avalanches. High elevation ski areas are also prone to heavy winds. Both the risk of avalanches and heavy winds can disrupt or interrupt ski operations.

- From an economic standpoint, extending existing ski areas to higher elevations is expensive. Mathis et al. (2003), who carried out a survey of projected ski area developments in Switzerland, found that the high mountain extensions would cost between CHF 40-49 million.

- High-elevation mountain environments are particularly fragile, and any initiatives to move ski areas into such environments are likely to face opposition from public and environmental groups.

2.3. Glacier skiing

Glacier skiing was originally developed as a niche market for *summer* skiing. However, the series of snow-deficient winters at the end of the 1980s demonstrated the significance of glaciers for winter skiing. While the ski areas at lower elevations suffered from the lack of snow, those resorts with access to glaciers could provide both an early start to the ski season and reasonable snow conditions throughout the winter. Indeed, the glacier resorts were able to benefit from the unfavourable snow conditions in lower areas (see König and Abegg, 1997). After the snow-deficient winters at the end of the 1980s, the former director of the Swiss Tourism Federation Gottfried Künzi said: "It is questionable whether the glaciers should remain sacrosanct, if the projections of future climate change became true" (cited in Abegg, 1996). Indeed, there are several projects relying on a further development of high-mountain environments, in particular extension projects of existing (glacier) ski areas[6]. In the Austrian Tyrol, for example, the development of ski areas on the Pitztal and Kaunertal glaciers looks likely in the future. In May 2004 the "Landtag" of Tyrol modified the regulation concerning the protection of glaciers, which means that it is now possible to extend skiing domains onto glaciers on the basis of land planning projects linked to tourism. Whereas the development of new installations for glacier skiing was until now forbidden under a 1990 directive concerning the development of ski runs, this prohibition is no longer included in the regulation modified in 2004. The project developed in May 2004 plans to extend by 400 m upwards a skiing domain in the Kaunertal onto the Weissseeferner glacier, which at 3 520 m in altitude would create the highest ski station in Austria. In the Pitztal area, ski operators are hoping to extend the skiing area onto two glaciers situated further north, which would guarantee a better snow cover. The loosening of the regulations concerning the protection of glaciers in the Austrian Tyrol led to protests by environmental groups. These groups responded with a survey (more than 80% of Tyrolean population is against a further extension of glacier ski areas) and a campaign called "Hands off the glaciers" (Hasslacher, 2005).

Extending skiing areas to glaciers may not be sustainable over the medium to long-term as it is estimated that by 2050 about 75% of the glaciers in the Swiss Alps will have disappeared and that by 2100 the whole of the Alps could lose almost all of their glacier cover (further details provided in Chapter 1, section 3). This trend in the reduction of the size and numbers of glaciers is already apparent. In the 1970s, there were approximately 5150 glaciers in the European Alps covering an area of 2 909 km^2. Compared to the year 1850 when glaciers in the Alps covered an area of 4 474 km^2 about 35% of this area was lost by the 1970s and almost 50% by 2000, when glaciers covered only 2 272 km^2. Zemp *et al.* (in press) have estimated that glacier area change per decade between 1850 and 1973 was of 2.9% and that this rate increased to 8.2% between 1973 and 2000. This is not only a severe loss of "mountain aesthetic" but also a problem for glacier skiing in both summer and winter. For example in Switzerland, a new ski lift was inaugurated on the south-facing Hockengrat glacier (in Lötschental,

---

[6]   Several examples from Austria are listed on the Osterreichischer Alpenverein website (www.alpenverein.at) (see Naturschutz, Alpine Raumordnung, Skierschliessungsprojekte).

Canton of Valais) at the end of 2003, but only a year later the opening of the 2004 winter ski season had to be delayed due to insufficient snow on the glacier[7]. This example illustrates the problems that glacier ski resorts could face in the future.

A new area of conflict between ski area operators and nature conservationists is about to emerge. As a result of the accelerated recession of Alpine glaciers in recent years, notably the record warm summer of 2003, ski areas have begun to install white sheets to protect the ice from radiation and restrict melting during summer. In Austria, there is an ongoing research project called "Aktiver Gletscherschutz – Active Glacier Protection" (Fischer *et al.,* 2006). Preliminary results from a test site at 2 950 m showed that considerable amounts of snow and ice (approximately 150 cm) could be prevented from melting.

In Tyrol, 28 hectares are covered by white sheets. This is about 3% of glacier ski area, or 1‰ of total glacier area. Examples from Switzerland demonstrate the variety of applications that these sheets can be used for (Schmid, 2006). The sheets are being used to protect critical parts of ski runs on glaciers (*e.g.,* Saas Fee and Verbier, Canton of Valais/Wallis), to protect the fixing of lifts masts on glaciers (Engelberg, Central Switzerland), to cover a halfpipe (Laax, Canton of Grisons), and to secure the access from the mountain station to the glacier (Andermatt, Central Switzerland).

From the perspective of ski operators, active glacier protection is a useful technology. The white sheets are easy to install, can be used several times, are cheap (the sheets used in Switzerland – made out of polyester – cost CHF 4 per m^2) and seem to be effective. In addition, they facilitate ski run preparation at the beginning of the season, and may reduce snow-making requirements. Active glacier protection is therefore regarded as a cost-saving strategy. It is a different story, however, from the perspective of nature conservationists. Environmental groups such as Greenpeace and Pro Natura have expressed concerns regarding unrestricted use of such white sheets. They refer to the use of snow-making equipment in the Alps as an analogy of what might happen with the use of white sheets: while snow cannons were used on a limited basis at the beginning (operators promised to cover only critical parts of the ski area) they are now used extensively throughout the European Alps (some ski areas are fully covered by snow-making). Consequently, environmental groups are calling for a formalised process to obtain permission to install a white sheet on a glacier and for the development of uniform regulations concerning the use of these sheets, as regulations in Switzerland, at least, vary between cantons.

The protective white sheets, however, will not save the glaciers. In the short and medium term, winter glacier skiing will be challenged by a further recession of the glaciers causing costly problems such as insufficient snow cover at the beginning of the season (= increased snow-making requirements), unstable infrastructure (*e.g.,* the fixing of the lift masts), and restricted access. In the long run, several ski areas will no longer be glacier ski areas as glaciers continue to recede and disappear.

---

[7]   See AlpMedia website http://www.alpmedia.net.

2.4.   Snow-making

Snow-making is the most widespread adaptation strategy used by ski area operators (Elsasser and Messerli, 2001; Burki *et al.*, 2005). It is used to extend the operating season and to increase the range of climate variability and change a ski area can cope with. While artificial snow-making was initially viewed as a luxury and then a back up strategy, it now appears to be viewed as a necessity. A statement from Wolfgang Bosch, Director of the Association of German Cableways, reflects the ski operators' point of view: "Without snow – no skiing, without skiing – no competitive winter tourism"[8].

Table 4.   **The expansion and present use of snow-making equipment**[9]

Austria	In Austria, by 1991 there were already 127 communities equipped with 250 snow-making units, which covered 20% of all Austrian ski tracks, equivalent to 5 000 ha (Breiling, 1998). Today, 50% of the total skiable terrain (approximately 11 500 hectares) is covered by snow-making. The ski area operators spent 144 million Euro on new snow-making equipment in 2005 alone (Fachverband der Seilbahnen Österreichs, 2005).
Switzerland	In Switzerland, the area covered by snow-making increased from 1.5% (1990) to 18% of total skiable terrain (projected figure for the winter of 2006/07). This corresponds to 3 960 hectares (Felix Maurhofer, Seilbahnen Schweiz, pers. comm., July 25th 2006).
German Alps	In Bavaria, the area covered by snow-making increased from 323 hectares in 2000 to approximately 425 hectares in 2004 (ca. 360 hectares in Swabia and Upper Bavaria). This is about 11.5% of total skiable terrain (Bayerisches Landesamt für Umweltschutz).
French Alps	In the whole of France, the area covered by snow-making increased from 121 hectares in 1983/84 to 4 003 hectares in 2003/2004. At the same time, the number of ski areas using snow-making equipment increased from 25 to 187. In the French Alps, 3 222 hectares are covered by snow-making. This is about 15.5% of total skiable terrain in 2003/04 (www.tourisme.gouv.fr).
Italian Alps	The number of snow guns in Alto Adige/South Tyrol almost tripled from 1994 (511) to 2004 (1407) (Amt für Seilbahnen, 2006). From 1997 to 2002 the area covered by snow-making equipment in South Tyrol increased by 60% (CIPRA, 2004: 6). CIPRA estimated that 40% of the skiable terrain in Italy, equivalent to 9 000ha, is covered by snow-making (CIPRA, 2004).

---

[8]   Source: www.seilbahnen.de.

[9]   Information on the use of snow-making equipment in the European Alps is plentiful. However, the data stem from many different, sometimes contradicting sources. Some data refer to the number of snow guns, others to the amount of skiable terrain covered by snow-making. The comparability of the information is therefore not always given.

    CLIMATE CHANGE IN THE EUROPEAN ALPS — ISBN 92-64-03168-5 — © OECD 2007

Artificial snow-making was first used commercially in the United States during the 1950s. In Europe, the large scale use of artificial snow-making started later and only really began to develop from the 1980s onwards. An overview of the expansion and present use of snow-making equipment in the five different Alpine countries considered in this analysis is provided in Table 4, while Figure 7 illustrates the share of ski runs equipped with artificial snow-making facilities for each of the Alpine countries. According to Pröbstl (2006), the rapid expansion of snow-making in the Alps has been triggered by the need to secure and guarantee the revenues of the ski area operators, the success of the ski resorts by providing a "snow guarantee" and the timely holding of international ski competitions as required by the *Fédération Internationale de Ski* (FIS). A case study of the use of artificial snow-making in the French Alps is provided in Box 2.

Figure 7. **Distribution of ski runs equipped with artificial snow facilities in the European Alps**

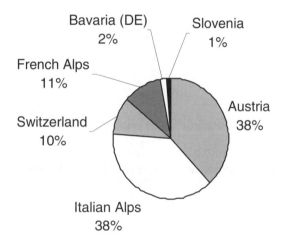

Source: CIPRA, 2004.

Box 2. Artificial snow-making in France

The first large scale use of artificial snow-making in France was in 1973 in Flaine, Haute Savoie with the use of snow cannons to cover a slope with a 600m drop and a surface area of 14 ha (ANPNC website). Since then, and especially since the early 1990s, there has been a significant investment in artificial snow cover by French ski resorts, with the aim of reaching a 'snow insurance' (Direction du Tourisme, 2004; Dubois & Ceron, 2003). There are currently 187 stations out of 308 in France that are equipped with artificial snow-making equipment (see Figure A.1. and A.2.).

Figure A.1 **Evolution of the number of French ski stations equipped with artificial snow-making equipment**

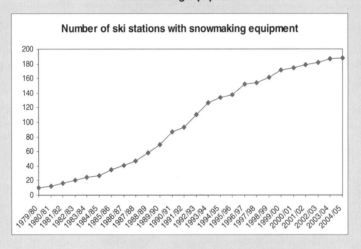

Figure A.2 **Evolution of the area covered with artificial snow and of installed power**

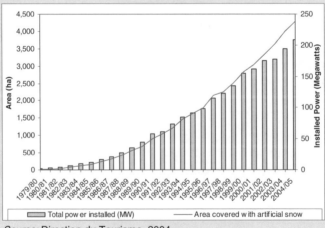

Source: Direction du Tourisme, 2004.

Box 2. continued on following page.

Box 2. Artificial snow-making in France (*continued*)

The ski stations in the French Alps represent the major users of artificial snow-making equipment with 72% of the French stations with artificial snow-making capacity found in the Alps. 81% of the area covered in artificial snow is also found in the Alps (see Table A). A total of 12 000 snow cannons are installed in France, with 8 480 (71%) in the French Alps alone.

Table A. **Area covered with artificial snow and total installed power for the Alps**

	Area covered with artificial snow (ha)	Installed Power (KWatts)
Alpes du Nord	2 339	115 403
Alpes du Sud	883	29 607
Total for the Alps	3 222	145 010
% of Total for France	80%	75%

Source: Direction du Tourisme, 2004.

For the 2003-2004 season, investment costs for snow-making material reached EUR 60 million for France of which EUR 45 million were in the French Alps alone. Table B provides the breakdown of investment costs for the two regions of the French Alps for 2003. The investment in new snow-making equipment, however, rarely represents the development of completely new installations but an extension to or improvement in current equipment. Functioning costs for that same season in France reached EUR 9.4million of which EUR 6.6million were in the French Alps.

Table B. **Investment costs for artificial snow-making equipment in the French Alps**

Region	Investment costs (million Euros)
Haute Savoie	8.24
Savoie	21.94
Isère et Drôme	6.1
Total for Alpes du Nord	36.28
Alpes du Sud	12.52
Total for the French Alps	48.8

Source: SEATM, 2003.

The costs of snow-making, however, are substantial, especially for small and medium-size stations. Hundreds of millions of Euros have already been invested in snow-making systems throughout the Alpine countries. For example, in France almost half a billion Euros were spent between 1990 and 2004 on artificial snow-making installations, while in Austria, approximately EUR 800 millions were spent on such installations between 1995 and 2003 (CIPRA, 2004). In Switzerland EUR 330 million have been invested to date in artificial snow-making installations (CIPRA, 2004).

The costs of snow-making can be divided into investment costs, operational costs, and maintenance costs. Different figures are available with regards to the production of one cubic metre of snow. For example, the Association of Austrian Cableways estimates the costs to be between one and five Euros while according to CIPRA (2004) the costs are between three and five Euros. The installation of a snow-making system in Austria costs EUR 25 000 to 100 000 per hectare [10], while in Switzerland it is estimated at EUR 650 000 per km (Elsasser and Messerli, 2001; Elsasser and Bürki, 2002; Mathis *et al.*, 2003). CIPRA (2004) estimates that it costs on average EUR 136 000 to cover one hectare with artificial snow. The annual operating costs in Switzerland vary between EUR 19 000 and 32 000 per kilometre (i.e. CHF 30 000 and 50 000). For example, in the canton of Valais/Wallis in Switzerland the operational costs of a snow-making system were estimated at EUR 33 000 (CHF 52 000) per kilometre. However, there is only a small difference of about EUR 2 000 between normal and snow-deficient winters. On average, the ski area operators spend 8.5% of their revenue on operating and maintaining the snow-making system (CIPRA, 2004).

While snow-making has the potential to offset the impact of climate change on the natural snow-reliability of ski areas, there clearly are both physical and economic limits to the extent to which this can be done. Snow-making also poses environmental externalities in terms of energy and water consumption, and ecological impacts. Currently the majority of snow cannons need ambient temperatures of -2 °C or less to be effective. Additives (such as Snowmax) can raise the ambient temperature threshold to 0 °C, but that poses a physical limit nevertheless. Furthermore, while the manufacturers of snow additives emphasise that additives do not pose any environmental consequences, a recent review of literature by Rixen *et al.* (2003) adopts a more cautious approach. This review concludes that although some studies found no effects of snow additives, others showed impacts (albeit on an inconsistent basis) on plant growth. The authors therefore recommend further investigation and longer-term studies on the ecological consequences of the use of snow additives prior to drawing definitive conclusions.

From an economic perspective the cost of snow-making will increase disproportionately under warmer temperatures as not only would more quantities of snow be required, but it will need to be produced under higher ambient temperatures. Energy costs already represent the largest share of total snow-making costs [in France energy represents 46% of the total costs of snow-making (Direction du Tourisme, 2004)], so an increase in these costs will represent a significant increase in total snow-making costs. The use and costs of snow-making will also not be spread evenly throughout the season, as certain periods such as the early season, will require more artificial snow production due to a likely decline in snow cover and will require further investments in snow-making technologies due to the warmer temperatures during those periods (Scott *et al.* in press).

The increased production of artificial snow will also require increased water withdrawal. Communities and environmental organisations have expressed their concern about water consumption associated with snow-making. The water use depends, amongst other things, on the climatic conditions, the efficiency of the snow-making system and, of course, the size of the area covered by snow-making. As a

---

[10] www.seilbahnen.at.

rule of thumb, 1 m^3 of water is equivalent to approximately 2 – 2.5 m^3 of snow. 70 to 120 litres per square metre are therefore necessary to produce snow cover suitable for skiing (20 to 35 cm) (Pröbstl, 2006). Table 5 shows the water consumption of a snow-making system in Garmisch-Partenkirchen, Bavaria, for the coverage with artificial snow of an area of 40 m wide and 1.1 km long with a snow depth of 25 cm using four snow guns and producing a total of 11 000 m^3 of snow. The table illustrates the increased water use required at warmer temperatures.

Table 5. **Water consumption of a snow-making system in Garmisch-Partenkirchen (Germany) under ambient temperature**

	–4 °C	–7 °C	–10 °C
Snow capacity per snow gun	23 m^3/h	34 m^3/h	45 m^3/h
Water use per snow gun	11 m^3/h	15 m^3/h	18 m^3/h
Operating time	120 h	81 h	61 h
Total water consumption	5 261 m^3	4 853 m^3	4 400 m^3

Source: Adapted from (Pröbstl, 2006).

According to a study carried out for the 2002/2003 winter season in France, on average 4 000 m^3 of water were needed to cover one hectare of a ski run that year (Direction du Tourisme, 2004). According to CIPRA (2004), to cover all of the 23 800 ha of ski runs in the Alps which have artificial snow-making equipment installed, 95 million m^3 of water would be needed per year to make the artificial snow. This amount of water corresponds to the annual water consumption levels of a town of 1.5 million inhabitants (CIPRA, 2004).

The increasing use of snow-making equipment in the last decade is directly leading to an increase in the demand for water. In the French Alps, for example, water consumption associated with snow-making increased from 3.7 million m^3 in 1994/95 to 10.6 million m^3 in 2003/04[11]. When water is withdrawn from natural sources such as rivers and lakes, water levels may be reduced at critical times of the year, impacting aquatic life (CIPRA, 2004; Pröbstl, 2006). In winter, a lot of water is bound in snow and ice, and therefore not available for snow-making. Pumping the water from afar is expensive. Occasionally, the water has to be cooled, sometimes also purified, adding to the costs. Water can also be withdrawn from drinking water reserves, although this can lead to disruption in the water supply system (which has already happened in some ski resorts). In order to secure the water supply for snow-making, many mountain reservoirs or artificial lakes have been built in recent years. However, not only does the construction of such reservoirs involve high costs, but it can also be very destructive on the environment and lead to "scars" on the Alpine landscape, as new roads have to be built to facilitate access to those altitudes, especially during the construction of the

---

[11]   www.tourism.gouv.fr.

reservoirs. Mountain reservoirs built at high altitudes are also vulnerable to flooding, rockfalls and avalanches, and these risks need to be taken into account especially if climate change results in an increase in such natural hazards.

Other environmental and ecological impacts of artificial snow-making are coming under increasing scrutiny. The impacts of ski piste preparation on Alpine vegetation are related to the compaction of the snow cover, namely the induction of soil frost, the formation of ice layers, mechanical damage, and a delay in plant development. These lead to changes in plant species composition and a decrease in biodiversity. The use of artificial snow modifies some of these impacts (cf Cernusca *et al.*, 1990; Kammer, 2002; Rixen *et al.*, 2003; Wipf *et al.*, 2005; and Pröbstl, 2006). The soil frost is mitigated due to an enhanced insulation of the snow pack. The formation of ice layers is hardly changed whereas the mechanical impacts of snow-grooming vehicles are mitigated because of a deeper snow cover. Later snowmelt leads to a further delay in plant development and, in addition, artificial snowing increases the input of water and ions to ski runs, which can have a fertilising effect and change the composition of plant species. Wipf *et al.* (2005) conclude: "Whether the impact of artificial snow on Alpine vegetation is considered positive or negative depends on the current state of the vegetation and the environmental objectives of a specific ski resort. If mechanical disturbance through snow-grooming vehicles or ski edges is a major problem, the increased protection afforded by artificial snow can be considered beneficial. However, in the case of endangered habitats poor in nutrients, like oligotrophic fens or nutrient-poor grasslands, the additional nutrient input by melt water of artificial snow is clearly a negative impact." Other concerns in connection with artificial snow production are the impact of noise on humans and the impact of noise and light on Alpine fauna (Pröbstl, 2006). A study in a German ski resort found that the start of ski operations in December led to a sudden change in habitat choice and diurnal activities of many wild animals (CIPRA, 2004). The noise generated by snow cannons is considerable, varying between approximately 60 dB and 115dB, which is comparable to the noise generated on high traffic roads (CIPRA, 2004).

The use of snow-making equipment is unevenly regulated across the Alpine countries, as there is no common legislation to all Alpine countries governing the use of artificial snow-making in the Alps. The Alpine Convention did consider this issue but did not manage to adopt wording that could be agreed to by all parties concerned. This has resulted in regulations differing from country to country, sometimes even within countries. The processes that are regulated concern the withdrawal of water, the construction of the snow-making system (*e.g.*, environmental assessment) and the operation of the snow-making system (*e.g.*, time of operation during night hours). The current government legislations concerning the use of artificial snow-making equipment in France, Germany, Italy, Austria and Switzerland are reviewed in Box 3.

With ski operators pushing for an increase in the development and use of artificial snow-making equipment, environmentalists are becoming concerned about an unlimited use of such equipment in the future. For example, in 2004 the first snow cannons on glaciers in France were installed on the Tignes glacier at an altitude of 3 000 m. Since then the resort of Val d'Isère has followed suit and the resort of Alpe d'Huez is now planning on using artificial snow on its glacier (Mountain Wilderness, 2005). These snow cannons were installed in order to enable the continuation of summer skiing.

Box 3. Government legislation concerning the use of artificial snow-making

In France specific regulations concerning the use of artificial snow-making equipment do not exist. The regulations applied are those that relate to the changes caused by the installation and use of such equipment (*e.g.*, construction of a "snow factory", withdrawal of water from natural surroundings, use of air compressors and expansion of the ski area). Water policing regulations, for example, are applied to water withdrawal installations in natural surroundings and work undertaken in the river/stream bed. These regulations require that a minimum rate of flow be maintained in watercourses and can ensure that any developments are subject to constraints relating to the protection of drinking water resources. The snow-making equipments that contain air compressors are subject to the regulations on classified installations, and the compressors are subject to checks every 3 years relating to the risk of deterioration of the equipment. Some laws, such as the Law on nature conservation, can require that the equivalent of an environmental impact assessment be performed before the installation of artificial snow-making equipment is authorised.

In Germany the only applicable legislation appears to be those concerning water regulations, which control the withdrawal of underground and surface water. Under these regulations the damage that might be caused to the natural balance and harmony of the countryside is discussed. Bavaria was known for its relatively strict regulations (Bayerisches Landesamt für Umweltschutz). Recently, however, these regulations were loosened. It is easier to get an approval now, and the ski area operators are allowed to make snow earlier and later in the season. The use of snow additives, however, is prohibited.

In Austria regulations concerning the use of artificial snow-making equipment vary between provinces and issues surrounding water resources are taken into account to a greater or lesser degree depending on the province.

In Italy the region of South Tyrol has developed specific regulations concerning artificial snow-making. Before an artificial snow-making installation can be built, an assessment has to be conducted by the Forestry authorities and the Commission for the Protection of the Countryside. An authorisation from the hydraulic works authorities is also required if state-owned water resources are used.

In Switzerland, at the federal level, the law on territorial development makes new buildings and installations subject to approval by the competent authorities. Snow cannons are also subject to an environmental impact study under the Federal Act on the Protection of the Environment concerning snow-covered areas of more than 5 ha. Entire slopes located below 1600m and areas (even restricted) located below 1200 m may not be covered with artificial snow. In addition, snow cannons may only be used as long as it is still possible to ski on the other slopes in the resort. In effect, this prevents ski operators from prolonging the season through the use of artificial snow. Regulatory differences also exist across the cantons, and the Association of Swiss Cableways has also adopted a number of principles aimed at limiting the use of snow cannons.

However, it is important to bear in mind the constraints concerning costs (as outlined earlier) and regulations. Even where snow-making is climatically feasible and water supply can be secured, the additional costs associated with large increases in snow-making volumes (additional infrastructure and operational costs) and making snow at higher average temperatures may be uneconomic to some ski area operators. It is also likely that many of the small and medium size resorts will not be able to afford the increased costs involved. The reservations that persist about the use of snow cannons are further supported by the resolution agreed by the International Commission for the Protection of the Alps (CIPRA) in May 2006 which cautions against the use of snow cannons, stating that they doubt that "quick-fix measures such as snow guns, which deal merely with the symptoms, are sustainable adaptation strategies for climate change".

3. Behavioural adaptations: operational practices, financial tools and new business models

This section examines the different types of behavioural adaptations, ranging from operational practices and financial tools to new business models and a move towards the diversification of activities. The use of some of these adaptations, however, appears to date to be fairly limited in the European Alps.

3.1. Operational practices

Operational practices involve a change in the way the ski operators manage the running and timing of the ski season. For many ski areas throughout the Alps, the season prior to the Christmas – New Year holiday break represents a low proportion of annual skier visits. Under climate change, with decreasing natural snow-reliability and increasing costs of additional snow-making, this relatively insignificant part of the season may no longer be economically viable. This would lead to (further) changes in the timing of season openings – a phenomenon already in evidence in some small- and medium-size ski resorts at lower elevations. Operators could also choose to intensify the use of a ski area by raising the lift capacity or limiting the slope availability to concentrate snow-making resources. Nevertheless increased utilisation levels will only prove effective (higher turnover, reduced operation costs) if skier satisfaction can be maintained.

Artificial, non-snow surfaces may also be an option for ski operators for very localised and specific uses. Such surfaces were first developed in the 1970s but have improved since then to the extent that they provide reasonable gliding and edging properties that do not damage ski equipment. Although the technology is little used currently, there may be niche applications on ski slopes in the future, for example as a surface in high traffic ski areas (*e.g.*, under ski lifts) or on small practice slopes and snowboarding parks. In Bavaria there were even plans (although these not have yet been carried out) to create a small "summer ski area" over two hectares of non-snow surface at an altitude of 1 000 m.

3.2. Financial instruments

Snow insurance and weather derivatives are potentially important financial tools which are available to ski area operators. The objective of the purchase of weather derivatives is to protect ski areas/ski resorts from financial loss due to the lack of snow. A weather derivative is a contract between two parties that stipulates the payment that will be exchanged as a result of the meteorological conditions during the contract period (Zeng, 2000). Weather derivatives are highly flexible instruments that can be based on a range of meteorological parameters and temporal periods. For example, a ski area could establish a weather-derivative contract based on snow depth in the critical Christmas – New Year period. By buying such a contract ski operators could minimise potential losses due to inadequate snow. However, to provide efficient and flexible risk transfer, these instruments require reliable weather data and buyers and sellers facing negatively correlated risks and therefore willing to trade over the same weather index and the same period of time. In the case of the Alps, where weather conditions can vary literally from one valley to the next, it may be difficult to find enough actors with negatively correlated risks to the same weather index. Therefore, the transaction costs of setting up such contracts may offset the potential benefits.

Snow insurance is another option. A snow insurance policy can be purchased that would hedge against the financial loss if far less than average snow fell during the season. Such products are available, from time to time also requested, but seldom used in the ski industry. In the US, for example, the Vail Resorts ski corporations in Colorado purchased snow insurance for the 1999-2000 ski season and were eventually paid US$ 13.9 million when low snowfall affected skier visits (Scott, 2006). However, since then, insurance premiums have increased substantially – possibly indicating adaptation of this insurance product by the financial sector – and large ski corporations, such as Intrawest and Vail Resorts, no longer hold weather insurance because of the high premiums (Scott, 2006).

Weather derivatives and snow insurance can provide ski resorts with a greater flexibility to experiment with marketing incentives to overcome skiers' reluctance to book a ski holiday because of uncertain snow conditions. If the ski area fails to open a certain percentage of the slopes, for example, a reduction is granted. In combination with weather derivatives and/or snow insurance, this marketing strategy may become an interesting option. The general trend in tourism, however, is towards shorter travel planning timeframes (*e.g.*, last-minute bookings). A flexible ticket price policy in accordance with the number of lifts running is another option. This is a widespread strategy of Australian ski resorts (König, 1998).

Snow-reliability, a major asset, is increasingly used as a marketing tool. The ski resorts refer to their snow-making capacity (*e.g.*, 100% snow guarantee), they promote the altitudinal range of their ski areas, carrying the prominent features even in their names, *e.g.*, "Isola 2000" which refers to high elevation of the bottom station, or "Zillertal 3000" which refers to the top of the ski area. In the winter of 2005/06, Switzerland started to internationally promote winter tourism by saying that there is no other country in Europe with 29 ski areas reaching higher than 2 800 m.

3.3. *Financial support*

There are many ways in which ski areas can be financially supported. Local authorities make single or annual contributions, grant loans or take a share in the business. Sometimes, they even run the ski area. State authorities have also been known to grant loans, usually at a very favourable rate or with no interest rate at all. These public funds are used to subsidise the operation, to cover deficits, and to pay for both the renewal and the extension of transport facilities. Increasingly, the money is used to fund snow-making requirements.

A few examples from Switzerland illustrate the importance of financial support by local and state authorities (Odermatt, 2005):

- The local authority of St. Moritz, Canton of Grisons, owns a few transport facilities in the ski areas. According to last year's budget, CHF 2.3 million were spent to run these facilities.

- In Melchsee-Frutt, Central Switzerland, the local authorities paid for a new chairlift incurring a total cost of CHF 8.5 million.

- In Gstaad, Bernese Oberland, about CHF 70 million are necessary to finance the renewal of existing transport facilities. The municipality of Saanen and the Cantons of Berne and Vaud will cover the "lion's share": CHF 39 and 28 million respectively.

In Flims-Laax-Falera, Canton of Grisons, a company was established to finance the additional snow-making requirements for the "Weisse Arena" ski area. The three communities concerned agreed – by public vote – to take a share of 80%. This is very beneficial from the ski area operator's point of view, as local authorities get better financial ratings than ski area operators (i.e. better conditions for the loans required) and the public is the one taking the risk. Interesting models to alternatively finance future investments are presented by Bieger and Laesser (2005).

An analysis of extension projects in Switzerland (1993 to 2001) showed that it was the Cantons that covered the largest part of the investment costs (42%), followed by the banks and the ski area operators themselves (21% each). Swiss Federation and local authorities only contributed 5% each to the investments (Mathis *et al.,* 2003). According to the authors, the Cantons pay great attention to regional economic criteria, while profitability, sustainable development and nature conservation seem to be less important. In addition, it appears that "the foreseeable consequences of climatic warming are not taken into consideration" (Mathis *et al.,*2003).

Under climate change, requests for financial support will likely increase. Ski areas will likely ask for additional help to secure their operations, insisting on their contribution to the local and regional economy. Furthermore, they will try to share the costs, particularly for snow-making. A growing number of ski area operators consider snow-making as a "public service" and therefore state that all those who benefit from snow-making should contribute to the costs – not only ski area operators, but also the accommodation industry and, most preferably, the whole community.

3.4. Co-operation and mergers

There are several forms and degrees of cooperation. A very common form of cooperation is the regional association, offering a single ski pass for several ski areas. This kind of cooperation can be found all over the Alps, even across national borders. Neighbouring ski area operators who are willing to cooperate may agree on joint marketing activities. They could share equipment (*e.g.*, snowcats) and personnel (*e.g.*, IT-specialists), benefit from better buying conditions and exchange know-how. Mergers represent another form of cooperation. They can aim at reducing market competition, cutting costs and/or increasing market share. A recent example was the merger of "Lenzerheide Bergbahnen Danis Stätz AG" and "Rothornbahn & Scalottas AG". The new company called "Lenzerheide Bergbahnen" is the third largest cableway company in the Canton of Grisons, Switzerland, with a total revenue of CHF 35 million. Looking ahead, the company managers would like to connect the ski area of Lenzerheide to the neighbouring resort of Arosa, arguing that only larger destinations will survive in the international market.

The motives behind cooperation and mergers are numerous, *e.g.*, competition, diversification, economies of scale, market share, and synergies. Bieger and Laesser (2005) published a list of potential synergies (better use of complementary resources) in the cableway industry. The authors conclude that loose cooperation is less effective than mergers and therefore favour fully integrated companies. However, the completion of a merger does not ensure the success of the resulting organisation. Problems may occur due to differences in, for example, corporate identity. Another option to improve the financial base of the company is vertical integration. Bieger and Laesser (2005) recommend that ski area operators should engage in activities other than their core business, such as ski rental and accommodation. The next step would be a resort company, or a destination holding, offering everything from the booking to the travel back home, maybe even in different locations/countries.

An interesting business model developed in North America is the ski resort conglomerate (Scott, 2006). Some companies have acquired ski areas in different locations across North America. Although not intended as climate adaptation, the conglomerate business model may prove to be one of the most effective adaptations to future climate change. The ski conglomerate provides greater access to capital and marketing resources, thus enhancing adaptive capacity, but also reduces vulnerability to the effects of climate variability and future climatic change through regional diversification in business operations. When poor conditions occur, the financial impact can be spread out through the organisation, and above average economic performance in one or more regions could buffer losses in another. Companies with ski areas in a single region or independent ski areas – that is the typical Alpine ski area – are at greater risk to poor climate conditions.

3.5. Winter revenue diversification

Winter sports, in particular skiing and snowboarding, but also cross-country skiing, remain the main attraction of Alpine resorts during wintertime. However, there are many people who ski only occasionally. There is, also, an increasing number of people visiting the resorts who do not ski at all. According to the president of Ski France an average skier is skiing about four hours per day, and that one out of four visitors in French winter sports resorts does not ski at all (Guillot, 2006). An even more pronounced pattern was found in Italy where 48% of visitors to winter sports resorts neither ski nor snowboard (WWF Italia, 2006a). On the Rigi, a famous mountain in Central Switzerland, the winter clientele has changed considerably. In the 1980s, it was almost exclusively skiers. However, last winter 65% of visitors were winter hikers, 15% were tobogganing, and only 20% were skiing. In fact, non-skiers represent an important and growing market at ski resorts.

Many resorts have made substantial investments to cater for the growing market of non-skiers. The most popular activities are winter hiking (more than 2 500 km of groomed trails in Switzerland only), tobogganing (approximately 500 toboggan runs in Austria), and snowshoeing (countless opportunities all over the Alps). The problem, of course, with these non-ski related activities is that they also require snow (although maybe less than downhill skiing). They may attract additional visitors but they do not aim to reduce the snow-reliance of Alpine winter resorts, which is the challenge under climate change, especially for low-lying resorts. In addition, many resorts, especially larger ones, offer a diversified tourism product including spas, health clubs, indoor sports, concerts, festivals, exhibitions and a variety of bars, restaurants and retail stores. These offers provide alternative activities for skiers and non-skiers alike. People take advantage of these offers and might even expect such a wide variety of products, but usually they do not visit the resort because of these "complementary" offers but because of the snow-related activities.

There is room for more non-snow related offers (*e.g.*, health tourism, congress tourism) and there are also successful niche-products on the market (*e.g.*, the humour festival in Arosa, Switzerland) but the potential for diversification should not be over-estimated:

- The above-mentioned offers are not directly dependent on snow. Indirectly, however, snow can play an important role in the process of choosing, for example, a congress location.

- Climate change scenarios also indicate wetter winters. More precipitation in combination with an increasing number of cloudy days may also reduce the attractiveness of non-snow related activities.

- Hoteliers, restaurant owners etc. who cater for all tourists are more likely to benefit from diversification than ski area operators who depend heavily on the transportation of skiers.

- Tourism managers from the Canton of Grisons, Switzerland, estimated that 20% of current-day visitors could be attracted by non-snow related offers (Abegg, 1996).

It therefore seems unlikely that the snow-related activities can be replaced entirely by non-snow related offers. Non-snow related offers play an important role, as they add to the variety of offers available and they support the winter business. However, they are not able to carry the winter industry. For the time being, there is no activity available that could substitute the revenue-generating power of traditional winter sports, in particular skiing.

3.6. All year tourism

Many resorts heavily rely on one single season: winter. This business model can be very perilous because of present climate variability (snow-deficient winters) and the potential impacts of projected climate change. In order to reduce the dependence on snow conditions, an enhanced engagement in year-round tourism is often recommended. This includes summer tourism (including the shoulder seasons) but also climate and weather independent offers such as congress, educational and health tourism. The objectives of this strategy are to back up the business and to reduce the snow-reliance of the resorts.

An interesting initiative (see Simon, 2006) is taking place in the *Département d'Isère* in France. Ski areas in this part of the French Alps, especially the smaller ones with inadequate facilities, cannot compete with their larger counterparts. The same ski areas are also rather susceptible to climate change. In order to be prepared for the future, the *Conseil Général* (regional government) decided to financially support diversification in tourism through the elaboration of "contracts for a diversified development" (*Contrats de Développement Diversifié*). The financial means are used, for example, to improve the quality of already existing (summer) products, to develop new offers particularly for families, and to pay for the deconstruction of old ski facilities. However, part of the money still goes into ski tourism. Box 4 details this and other related initiatives that are taking place in the Rhône Alpes Region.

Box 4. Policies supporting diversification initiatives in the Rhône Alpes Region, France

In the *Départements* of Savoie, Haute Savoie and Isère there is a move to support of the diversification of tourism activities in ski resorts. In Savoie, the *Département* has announced its intention to develop tourism during all four seasons and to diversify tourism facilities in order to counter the single industry phenomenon and cope with changing demand. This determination is not prompted by any fear of insufficient snow; rather, it reflects the need to anticipate climate change. In the *Département* of the Isère where there are numerous medium-altitude resorts whose activities are threatened by climate change, the *Département* is clearly determined to help them give fresh impetus to their tourism sector and diversify their activities by developing active policies at the departmental level to support medium altitude resorts (Interview with Le Scan, 2004). The instruments used to develop the diversification policies are the "*Contrats Stations Moyennes*" at departmental level and the "*Contrats de Plan Etat Region*" (CPERs) at regional level. The aim of the *Contrats Stations Moyennes* is to promote the development of medium altitude resorts with over 2000 beds for tourists. These contracts are designed to encourage the emergence of projects which are economically realistic and sustainable at local level. The CPERs are individually tailored to the requirements of each resort and the funding for these contracts is allocated for marketing schemes and capital requirements with the main aim of expanding summer tourism above all. Contracts for a Diversified Development (*Contrats de Développement Diversifié* or CDDs) have also been put in place at departmental level. Depending on the vulnerability of resorts to a lack of snow, the aim of these contracts is to help these resorts to either boost their snow-related activities or reduce them by backing commune diversification projects.

An example of the use of CDDs can be found in the *Département* of the Isère where the General Council has committed technical and financial resources to the introduction of a new policy aimed at diversifying tourism activities in mountain regions. In 2001 a study investigating tourism in the Isère was carried out and recommended that development and diversification plans should be launched. In 2003 the General Council acted on the study's conclusions and proposed diversification scenarios. Financial aid made available by the *Département* is designed to promote the diversification of activities (aid in assessing tourism potential and seeking new activities), to help with the decision to abandon snow-related activities in resorts with the least snow, to improve facilities such as accommodation and transport and to promote tourism-related activities.

As part of the 2000-2006 CPER the Rhône-Alpes Regional Council renewed its "*entreprise-station*" initiative (first launched in 1995) for the period 2000-2006 with the main theme being medium-altitude resorts. The "*entreprise-station*" project consists of either drawing up or continuing with – as the case may be – a summer and winter strategy specific to the resort, which both optimises the resort's internal management and promotes the marketing of what it has to offer. Under CPERs, aid is made available (both by the State and the Regions) which can be used by the local authorities and management structures responsible for the eligible resorts.

There are also CPER and European Union-financed 'Mountain Contracts' which aim to develop regional tourism potential by diversifying the range of activities over the year (all year tourism), strengthening a territory's specific features and improving accommodation and transport.

Alpine summer tourism depends on "good" weather. In comparison to the stable conditions of the Mediterranean, the Alpine summer weather is rather variable, leading to lower degrees of weather satisfaction by tourists. However, this perception may change in the future, with regional climate scenarios projecting warmer and drier summers in Europe. Summers on the Mediterranean may become too hot whereas the temperatures at higher elevations – accompanied by less precipitation – remain comfortable. A potential analogue is the very hot summer of 2003 (and partly also in 2006) when inhabitants from the lowlands surrounding the Alps fled to the mountains to temporarily seek relief from the heat. However, climate change will also have negative impacts on Alpine summer tourism, with the continued retreat of glaciers (see Chapter 1, section 3) which will severely affect the attractiveness of the mountain environment. The loss of "mountain aesthetic" will be accompanied by the disappearance of tourist attractions such as ice caves and, presumably, the remaining summer ski areas. In addition, climate change will increase the melting of permafrost and will make some mountain areas more vulnerable to landslides. Cableway stations, lift masts and other buildings on permafrost soil may become unstable (Haeberli, 1992), and considerable amounts of money will be required to re-fit them. Hiking and climbing could be more dangerous because of increasing rock fall (Behm et al., 2006). And white water activities like river rafting may become less attractive due to lower water levels in Alpine rivers.

Again, hoteliers and restaurant owners are more likely to benefit from seasonal diversification than cableway operators. In Switzerland, summer tourists only spend 7.9% of daily holiday budget on transportation, whereas in wintertime it is 22.9% (Seilbahnen Schweiz, 2005a). In the past, only cableway operators who provided access to a famous peak were able to earn money in summer. Some companies reduced or stopped summer operation, while others threatened to cease operation until the resort community agreed to contribute to the operating costs (e.g., Sportbahnen Vals AG in the Canton of Grisons, Switzerland). The cableway operators try to stimulate demand by catering for specific customer groups such as mountain bikers and paragliders. Additionally, they invest in gastronomy, themed walks, adventure parks and summer toboggan runs to increase the number of families, hikers and sightseers. For example, Swiss cableway companies currently operate 21 summer toboggan runs (19 in the Alps). After the snow-deficient winters at the end of the 1980s, a number of companies started to think about a larger engagement in summer alternatives, and for quite a few, summer tobogganing was top priority. As a consequence, the number of summer toboggan runs rapidly increased, but not all of them turned out to be successful (Mathis et al., 2003). Success depends – among other factors – on effective market research, which investigates the potential demand, the attractiveness of the product and the marketing power available to make the product known.

3.7. Withdrawal from ski tourism

Ski areas at lower elevations, where economic survival has been jeopardised by the mild winters of the past, may actively engage in downsizing or quitting ski tourism. Usually, such areas cannot rely on favourable natural conditions, and they hardly have the possibility (*e.g.*, altitudinal range) and/or the financial means to invest, for example, in snow-making equipment. In addition, financial institutions are only prepared to grant very restrictive loans to these ski areas. For example, Swiss Banks now only provide very restrictive loans to ski areas at altitudes below 1 500 m (Elsasser and Burki, 2002), while some banks in Canada are known to have discussed the implications of climate change when carrying out financial negotiations with ski resorts (Scott *et al*, in press). Opinions among tourism representatives differ a great deal, whether such ski areas should be retained at all, and if so, how the future operation could be guaranteed and financed. Some argue that a certain downsizing of the industry is necessary, and that non-profitable ski areas should be dismantled. Others, on the other hand, believe in an obligation to retain these ski areas, particularly for regional economic reasons (Elsasser and Bürki, 2002).

The small ski area at the Gschwender Horn in Immenstadt, Bavaria, provides a famous and successful example of an actively planned withdrawal from ski tourism. At the beginning of the 1990s, after a series of snow-deficient winters, the municipality, together with the Allianz Umweltstiftung, decided to withdraw from the non-profitable ski operation. The facilities (two ski lifts and a transportable children's lift) were dismantled, the ski runs (approximately 40 hectares) re-naturalised. Today, the area is used for summer and winter tourism, namely hiking, mountain biking, snowshoeing and ski touring (see Allianz Umweltstiftung, 2005).

There are other projects, for example the "Gemeindenetzwerk Ökomodell Achental e.V." (Community Network Eco-Model Achental). This international network established a free coach service to transport the skiers from eight different communities in Bavaria and Tyrol to the most snow-reliable ski resort within the network area. Ski resorts at lower elevations refrain from extending their ski areas and concentrate on eco-tourism (Neuhäuser, 2006). Another idea is the establishment of a fund to financially support the active withdrawal from ski tourism, *e.g.*, for dismantling the facilities. It is likely that such ideas (and many others) will become more prevalent under climate change.

4. Discussion and policy implications

Climatic changes are already having a significant impact on winter tourism in the European Alps, and anticipated changes are expected to cause significant further decline in the snow-reliability of Alpine ski areas. These impacts however are not uniform and will lead to "winners" and "losers", both in terms of regions (*e.g.*, Grisons, Valais, and Savoie are considerably less vulnerable compared to Alpes Maritime, Styria, and Friuli/Venezia/Giulia), and in terms of the ski areas themselves (with areas with high altitudinal range being considerably less vulnerable than low-lying ski areas). The winter tourism industry has responded to the implications of observed changes, and a range of technological and behavioural measures have been put into practice to offset the adverse impacts. Such adaptation measures, however, cannot be isolated from other business decisions and are influenced by a wide range of other factors namely market demand, competition and environmental regulations. The observed adaptations have also largely remained reactive and little evidence can be found that ski areas are engaged in long-term business planning in anticipation of future changes in climate.

For a number of reasons, climate change adaptation is also anticipated to remain largely individualistic at the level of ski operators. The availability of adaptation options will vary according to geographic characteristics (*e.g.*, available altitudinal range, local climatic conditions and distance to major markets), government jurisdiction (*e.g.*, tourism policy, environmental regulations and water access rights) and business models (*e.g.*, independent ski area operators versus ski conglomerates). In other words, adaptation will be very context-specific. Given the time horizon of projected climate change, winter tourism will not undergo a sudden, radical change. Climate change can be viewed as a catalyst that will reinforce structural change in the winter tourism industry by highlighting the opportunities and risks inherent in already existing, and future, tourism development. Ultimately it is the adaptive capacity (not climate) that will determine the future of the resorts under climate change.

This raises two critical issues for governments. The first relates to the degree of oversight and intervention that might be needed in what is, to a large extent, autonomous adaptation driven by market forces. One place where government role might be critical is with regard to the environmental and social externalities that might be created by the implementation (or over-implementation) of particular adaptation strategies. For example, snow-making has implications on water and energy consumption, the grooming of ski slopes can affect vegetation and reduce slope stability, while moving ski operations to higher altitudes can threaten fragile environments. Currently government policies in this regard vary considerably, both across and within countries. France and Germany currently do not have specific regulations regarding artificial snow-making, although some aspects are covered within existing regulations for water withdrawal. Austria meanwhile has explicit regulations, but they vary across provinces, while in Italy only South Tyrol has snow making regulations. In Switzerland, meanwhile, snow cannons are subject to an environmental impact assessment and there are specific regulations on where they can be used. Regulations vary similarly – or are absent entirely – for the use of snow additives, for grooming of ski slopes, and for moving ski activities to higher altitudes.

Yet another place where government and public policy might play a role is in providing an adequate safety net to those at the "losing" side of the adaptation equation. This is because climate change impacts on Alpine winter tourism have significant equity implications. Smaller resorts which also tend to be at low altitudes, are both more vulnerable to climate change and have fewer opportunities for expensive adaptations. Meanwhile ski conglomerates, which operate a number of resorts, have lower climate risk (as their ski areas often have greater altitudinal range), better diversification of risk, and access to greater technical and financial resources to adapt. It is likely that the larger ski resorts that maintain profitability and remain in operation will also be in a position to take advantage of a climatically altered business environment and to gain market share due to a reduction in competition because of other ski resorts going out of business. In terms of government responses there is, once again, considerable variation across the region, from *laissez faire* (let the market decide) to providing financial support to offset incurred damages. In particular, a key tension that governments and local communities need to confront jointly is between measures that tend to protect *status quo* for as long as possible and those which facilitate a smoother transition to the new realities of the changing climate. Overall, the current emphasis has been more on preserving the status quo and less so on transitions that might be economically and politically expensive.

Chapter 3

Climate change adaptation and natural hazards management

by

Simon Jetté-Nantel and Shardul Agrawala

Natural hazards are inherent to Alpine countries, have significant impacts on societies and economies, and are sensitive, to varying degrees, to climatic change. This chapter provides an overview of natural hazards and vulnerabilities in the Alpine arc and then discusses the implications of climate change adaptation for natural hazards management in Austria, France and Switzerland. In terms of vulnerability, many hazards which have strong linkages to climate change, such as hazards related to glaciers and permafrost areas, actually have relatively low/medium economic significance. On the other hand, hazards which have considerably higher economic and social significance, such as floods and windstorms, have more complex and less certain linkages with climate change. Hence, a multi-pronged approach is needed to take climate change risks into account when dealing with various natural hazards. Despite their very high adaptive capacities with regard to dealing with natural hazards, France, Switzerland and Austria face significant challenges in dealing with current hazards, let alone the implications of climate change. In addition to improving the efficiency of current hazard management, there is a need for more forward-looking approaches that also consider anticipated climate risks. Finally, in specific cases where climate-related risks are rapidly evolving or the impacts are already evident (as is the case for permafrost and glacial risks) an effective adaptation strategy would be to institute risk monitoring and risk reduction projects.

Besides winter tourism, climate change is also expected to have implications on the vulnerability to natural hazards in the European Alps. There are linkages of course between winter tourism and natural hazards. For example, any increase in the vulnerability of Alpine areas to natural hazards is likely to have direct implications on winter tourism infrastructure as well as the human settlements that serve as the base for such activities. On the other hand, there are some obvious differences between the two. While climate change has clearly discernible implications on the snow-reliability of ski areas, its implications on a diverse array of natural hazards that are already prevalent in the Alps are much more complex. Further, while adaptation measures in winter tourism have largely been autonomous, context-specific, and initiated primarily by the private sector, any responses to deal with the implications of climate change on natural hazards will almost certainly involve a greater role for public agencies, require much more co-ordination and planning, and would likely be superimposed on policies and measures that already exist in the various Alpine countries to deal with natural hazards. At the same time, the role of the private sector is also important, particularly through the insurance and re-insurance industry.

This analysis first provides an overview of natural hazards and vulnerabilities in the Alpine arc. Key weather and climate related hazards are discussed next, along with the potential implications of climate change. The next part of the analysis discusses the implications of climate change adaptation on natural hazards management in three Alpine countries: France, Switzerland, and Austria. The focus here is both on existing natural hazard management frameworks and insurance mechanisms, as well as any additional measures that might be required to address the emerging risks posed by climate change.

1.   Natural hazards in the Alps: overview and implications of climate change

Natural hazards are inherent to Alpine countries (Figure 8) and have significant impact on Alpine societies and economies, generating economic losses of EUR 57 billion over the 1982-2005 period (Figure 9). This is without counting the large investments made by Alpine countries in protection and prevention measures. These hazards are highly influenced by natural and climatic factors such as precipitation, temperature, slopes and biomass cover. Consequently, these hazards are sensitive, at various degrees, to climatic changes. In this report, five types of natural hazards are considered: floods, storms, mass movements, avalanches, and forest fires. They have been selected based on their impact on Alpine societies, as well as their sensitivity to climate.

Figure 8. **Disaster and loss events in the Alps, 1980-2005**

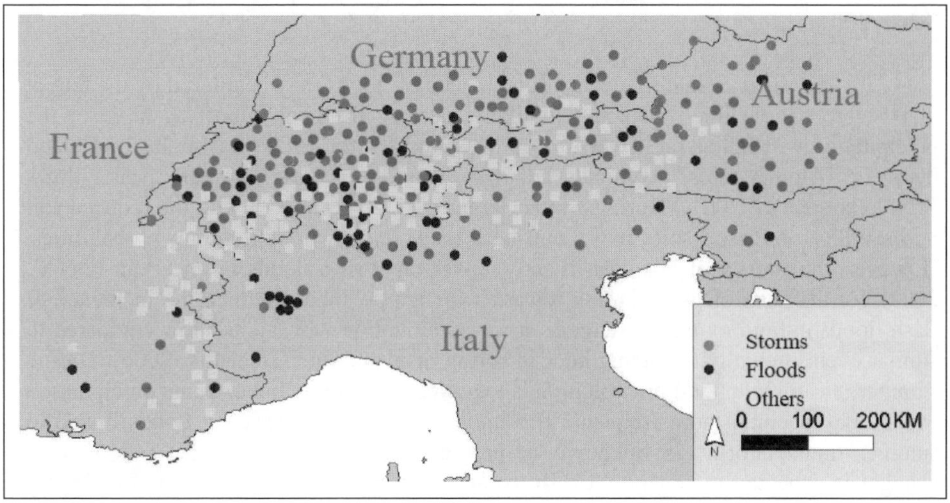

Source: Modified from a document provided by Munich Re, Geo Risks Research © 01/2006 NatCatSERVICE ®.

1.1. Floods

Floods are triggered by the interactions between extreme rainfalls, soil water saturation, and snow melt, causing streams to concentrate rapidly into high water volumes. In mountain regions, flash floods are sudden and violent phenomena which can carry materials such as wood, mud and stones. The velocity of these mountain events often creates bank erosion, increasing the concentration of debris within the water flow, and potentially leading to debris or mud flows. The lack of river maintenance, concreting of the riverbanks, and the waterproofing of urban areas also represent aggravating factors for floods.

Of all hazards in the Alpine regions, floods are creating the most economic damages (Figure 9), and many of the most densely populated Alpine areas have been hit severely by floods in recent years (Appendix 5). For flash floods, warning time is often short and evacuation is not always possible. The water flow and the large debris that floods may contain can destroy buildings, and infrastructures such as roads and railways, leading to perturbation in transportation. The deposition of smaller sediments also entails large cleaning costs and can damage crops. Floods can also cause major ecological impacts if chemical stocks are engulfed by water flows.

Currently, no cross-Alpine trends in the incidence of floods has been ascertained and it remains unsure whether particular extreme flood events (for example in Austria and Switzerland 2002, 2005) are entirely due to natural fluctuations or whether climate change may have been a contributing factor. Nevertheless, in terms of overall trends, a significant increase in winter and fall intense precipitation with return period of 30 days has been observed in many areas of the Swiss Alps for the 1901-1994 period (Frei and Schär, 2001).

Under climate change scenarios, incidence of floods may be altered by the retreat of the zero degree line[12], which will likely increase the peak runoff as more of the precipitation will fall as rain (OcCC, 2003). A study of the Rhine Basin also concluded that, in Alpine areas, climate change would increase winter peak flows (Middelkoop et al. 2001). During winter, larger rain fall combined with the reduced soil permeability of frozen soils may contribute to increase winter flooding probabilities. However, the impact of changes in snow cover on spring floods is uncertain (OcCC, 2003) but the shift of precipitation toward winter time should reduce the incidence of flash floods in high mountain range as more precipitation will fall as snow compared to similar events actually occurring later in spring or in summer (Beniston, 2006). During summer, meanwhile, total precipitation is expected to decrease but extreme precipitation events may become more frequent. The impact of climate change on floods linked to summer thunderstorms is unknown at present (OcCC, 2003). In the end, climate changes is expected to generate a shift towards winter precipitation leading to a higher incidence of floods in lowlands but a lower incidence in higher mountain ranges.

1.2. Storms

Most of the Alpine arc regions are exposed to the threat of winter storms such as Vivian and Lothar (1999). Storms can be highly damaging for properties, infrastructure and forests, leading to economic impacts particularly on the insurance and forestry industries. These storms are linked with intensive low-pressure systems, large temperature gradients, and the cyclonic activity occurring in the North Atlantic. However, the linkages with the NAO index have not been formally established so far (OcCC, 2003). On the other hand, summer storms affecting Alpine regions are often linked with the föhn[13] and tend to affect mainly the Northern Alps. Storms represent the second major cause of economic damages and the first cause of insured damages related to natural hazards within the Alpine arc (Figure 9). Extreme events have the largest impact as storm damages increase non-linearly with maximum wind speed (Klawa and Ulbrich, 2003).

---

[12] Altitude at which the temperature of zero degree is reached.

[13] The föhn is a warm, dry, and often strong wind affecting the northern Alps. A föhn can cause sudden and dramatic increases in the temperature within a few hours.

Figure 9. **Economic and insured losses due to natural hazards in the Alps, 1980-2005**

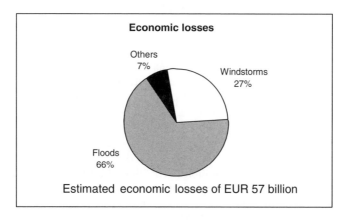

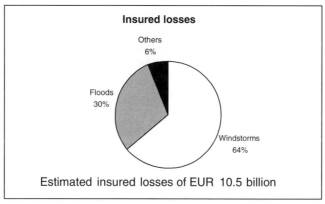

Source: Data provided by MunichRe, GeoRisk Research © 01/2006 NatCatSERVICE ®.

As a result of climate change, storms could be exacerbated by the changes in pressure and temperature gradients and the acceleration of circulation in the atmosphere. With respect to *föhn* storms, impacts of climate change are yet unclear (OcCC, 2003). But for winter storms, scenarios indicate that more intense storms are possible for Western Europe (OcCC, 2003). A recent study by SwissRe concluded that in Europe storms would increase in frequency and intensity. For Switzerland, the study suggests an average increase of 19% in annual economic loss over the 1975-2085 period (SwissRe, 2006).

1.3. Avalanches

Avalanches occur on steep slopes, and heavy snow fall in regions above 1200m of altitude is the main climatic factor affecting avalanche incidence (OcCC, 2003). Avalanches are induced by stability rupture in the snow cover, which can be triggered by vibrations coming from skiers, animals, or rock/serac falls. Avalanches can be extremely violent and cause extensive damages due to snow weight and volume, but also because of the various materials they transport (ice, rocks, trees, etc). The most affected regions are the high mountain areas, including the French and Swiss Alps, and western Austria. Avalanches have claimed an average of 100 victims per year in the Alps over the last 30 years (EEA, 2003). Victims are primarily skiers. Also, large avalanches can run for miles, and create massive destruction of the lower forest and inhabited structures. In the 19 cantons of Switzerland covered by public insurers, avalanches caused around EUR 70 million (CHF 110 million) in insured damages over the period 1995-2005[14]. Another example is the avalanche of Montroc, France, in 1999, where around 300 000 cubic metres of snow slid, killing 12 people, injuring another 20 and destroying 14 cabins (Glass *et al.*, 2000).

No clear trends have been identified in the frequency and number of avalanches in the Alps over the past century. In Switzerland, while a slow downward trend in snow cover was identified during the 1990s, the implications for the incidence of avalanches remain unclear. In some regions, especially at high altitudes, increasing winter precipitations under climate change conditions could increase the snow cover. If the frequency of heavy snowfall increases, then the risk of extreme avalanche may increase as well. At lower altitudes, the avalanche risk is not expected to increase (OcCC, 2003).

1.4. Mass movements

Mass movements, such as landslides, mudflows, and rock falls, involve the fall or slippage of large amounts of rock and/or soil. Some of these can be sudden, like small rockfalls and mudflows, while others provide clear precursory signs and take long periods to develop (*e.g.*, major rockfalls, deep seated landslides or creep). Most often mass movements occur as a result of slope instability and weathering, induced by phenomenon of dissolution and erosion. Soil water saturation due to heavy rainfall or snow melt is often a contributing factor to mass movements.

Mass movements can be threatening for humans and assets; while pebble falls may be deadly to humans, major rock falls can be destructive and affect buildings and infrastructures. In the 19 cantons of Switzerland covered by public insurers, mass movements caused above EUR 21 million (CHF 33 million) in insured damages over the 1995-2005 period[15]. Another mass movement phenomenon is the inflation-retreat of clay which is linked to droughts and causes damages to house foundations. In the

---

[14] Source: Intercantonal Reinsurance Union, www.kgvonline.ch.

[15] Source: Intercantonal Reinsurance Union, www.kgvonline.ch.

department of Alpes-Maritimes, France, this hazard has become the most expensive in recent years (Prudent, 2006).

Some current trends in the incidence of mass movements have been identified. In lower altitude (<2 200m) areas of the French Alps, the number of debris flows and the frequency of debris flows less than 400m in length have decreased significantly since the 1980s (Jomelli *et al.,* 2004). Linkages between mass movements and climate change are complex as various factors could affect their incidence. Increased winter precipitation, providing larger water supply, could decrease slope stability and lead to more frequent mass movements. But the ascent of the forest line could potentially stabilise some areas which were not previously covered. Under climate change scenarios, frequency and magnitude of landslides and debris flows are expected to increase due to more intense precipitations during summertime. Frequency of rockfalls is also expected to increase due to changes in the spring thawing process[16]. But the incidence of mass movement is not expected to evolve equally across Alpine regions. In the Southern Alps climate change will likely lead to slightly less mass movements as the effect of more intense precipitation is offset by a dryer climate (Bathurst *et al.,* 2005).

1.5. *Glacier and permafrost hazards*

The evolution of glaciers involve the movements of large masses of ice which can impose damages to infrastructure (*e.g.*, ski lifts), but changes in glacier systems can also lead to more disastrous events such as glacial lake outburst floods (GLOFs) or ice avalanches. The discharge of glacial lakes can also turn into debris flows. The evolution of glaciers also affects river flows during summer time as hot summers can lead to increased water flows from glacier melt. But, in the longer-term, glacier mass reduction would tend to reduce the summer river flows. On the other hand, rockfalls, and debris flows can originate from the destabilisation of rocks or debris in melting permafrost. Chain reactions and combinations of hazards, *e.g.*, rockfalls triggering GLOFs or avalanches, are also possible.

GLOFs are the most destructive hazards originating from glaciers due to the large water volume and large areas covered. Luckily, glacial lakes, from which GLOFs originate, usually form slowly and can be monitored (Kääb *et al.,* 2005). However, glacier lakes forming inside the glacier are not visible, are much less understood and more difficult to monitor. Ice avalanches are much more sudden but cover much smaller areas. However, these can trigger chain reactions which have farther reaching consequences.[17] The higher mountain ranges of Switzerland, France, and Italy are most affected by glacier hazards (see Figure 10).

At the global level, 30 to 50% of actual glaciers could disappear by 2100 given a warming of 2 to 4 °C (Beniston, 2003). Recent studies for the Swiss Alps indicate that

---

[16] Markus Stoffel, University of Fribourg, personal communication.

[17] Wilfried Haeberli, University of Zurich, personal communication.

almost all Alpine glaciers could disappear by 2100 given a warming of 5 °C (Zemp *et al.*, 2006). Incidence of GLOFs could increase as these warmer temperatures and glacial retreat favour the creation of glacial lakes. Under climate change scenarios "wide-spread rockfall and geotechnical problems with human infrastructure are likely to be recurrent consequences of warming permafrost in rock walls" (Gruber *et al.*, 2004). Overall, in glacier and permafrost areas, a warmer climate is expected to reduce slope stability and increase the risk of mass movements.

An increase in the number of mass movements in permafrost and glacial zones has been documented in some regions of the Alps. For example, the number of debris flows originating from glaciers has increased in the Canton de Valais, Switzerland (OcCC, 2003). The unusually hot summer of 2003 was associated with exceptional rockfalls due to the melting of ice-filled discontinuities (Gruber *et al.,* 2004). These hazards are directly linked to glacier and permafrost retreat, which are probably the most prominent signs of climate change. However, a recent study showed that frequency of debris flows originating from permafrost areas in Ritigraben (Swiss Alps) has been decreasing, although a lower frequency may also be associated with more intense events due to larger accumulation of materials between events (Stoffel and Beniston, 2006).

Figure 10. Casualties, glacial events and GLOFs in Austria, France, Italy and Switzerland
(all documented events, approx. 1600 to 2000)

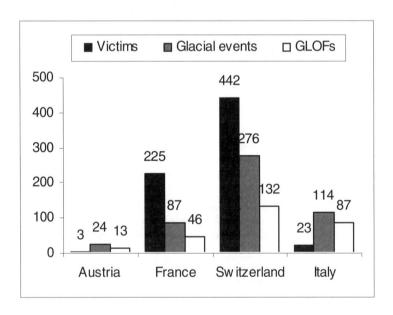

Source: http://glaciorisk.grenoble.cemagref.fr.

1.6.   Forest fires

Favourable conditions for forest fires are largely determined by climatic variables and biomass cover, the latter being also influenced by human activities. High temperatures, droughts, winds (*föhn*), and thunderstorms are all climatic factors directly linked to forest fires. However, human activity is often what triggers forest fires. The lower mountain ranges within the Southern Alps are the most affected regions due to climatic and environmental factors (FAO, 2001: OcCC 2003).

Obviously, forest fires directly affect forests and the industries linked to this resource, such as summer tourism and forestry industries. But areas of ecological interest are also affected. Buildings and infrastructures located along forests can also be damaged. Although victims are sometimes reported, in general evacuation and rescue plan allows their minimisation.

Climate change could increase fire risk significantly. Increasing trends have already been observed in some Alpine regions. Reinhard *et al.* (2005) showed that fire risk due to drought events increased over the 1971-2005 period in southern Swiss Alps. As well, in the Alpine area north of the Canton of Valais in Switzerland, the number of fires and the acreages affected increased in the 1990s by a factor of 3-4 in comparison to previous decades (OcCC, 2003). On the other hand, the department of Alpes Maritimes, the most affected region of the French Alps, displays a downward trend in terms of areas affected by forest fires over the 1973-2005 period[18]. Under climate change conditions, it is expected that the potential increase of summer storms could lead to an increase in the risk of forest fires. In the Southern Alps, expected temperature increase and potential increase in heavy winds and droughts would create more favourable fire conditions (OcCC, 2003).

2.   Synthesis of key vulnerabilities and implications for adaptation

The necessity of suitable adaptation measures to the implications of climate change on natural hazards depends both on the strength of the linkages between climate change and particular hazards, as well as the overall significance of the hazard itself. Based on the analysis in the previous section Table 6 provides a subjective summary of the linkages between particular hazards and climate change, as well as the geographic and economic significance of the hazards themselves.

As is evident from Table 6, many hazards which have strong linkages to climate change actually have relatively low/medium economic significance. The clearest impacts of climate change on natural hazards occur in glacial and permafrost zones. From a *national* perspective, the damages associated with these hazards have limited economic implications as the regions in which such impacts occur tend to be remote and sparsely populated. However, these damages are of much greater importance for *local* communities and can also have indirect negative consequences on the tourism industry.

---

[18]   Source: Promethee database, www.promethee.com.

On the other hand, hazards which have considerably higher economic and social significance, such as floods and windstorms, have more complex and less certain linkages with climate change. Despite the uncertainty of potential climatic change impacts on floods and winter storms, the risk related to these changes should be taken seriously given the economic importance of such events and the growing vulnerability of Alpine societies to these impacts on account of demographic, land-use and other pressures.

Table 6. **Climate change impacts on natural hazards in the Alpine Arc**

Changes in Natural Hazards	Confidence in projected changes	Most affected regions	Economic importance
Permafrost related hazards: Increase in frequency of rockfalls and magnitude of debris flows	Very high	High mountain range, tourism areas	Low
GLOFs: Increasing incidence of Glacial Lake Outburst Floods	Very high	High mountain range, tourism areas	Low
Other Glacier related hazards: Increasing frequency and magnitude	High	High mountain range, tourism areas	Low
Winter Floods: Greater intensity and frequency	Medium	Lower mountain range, densely populated areas	Very high
Storms: Greater intensity and frequency	Medium	Alpine arc, densely populated areas	Very high
Rockfalls: Increasing frequency	Medium	Lower to medium mountain range	Medium
Forest fires: Increasing number of events in Southern Alps	Medium	Lower mountain range of Southern Alps	Medium
Landslides and debris flows: Increasing frequency and magnitude	Medium/Low	Lower to medium mountain range	Medium
Avalanches: Increasing frequency and magnitude at high altitudes	Low	High mountain range, tourism areas	Medium

How best, then, to take climate change risks into account in dealing with natural hazards in the Alps? Clearly, based on the above discussion, a multi-pronged approach is needed. A natural place to start would be from the institutional structures and risk transfer mechanisms that already exist in the Alpine countries to deal with natural hazards. Climate change and its implications (even if uncertain) are one more reason to improve the efficiency of such structures and mechanisms. Second, climate change might also require making existing mechanisms forward-looking to take anticipated risks into account, as well as more flexible so that they can be more amenable to incorporate new information on evolving risks. Third, in specific cases where climate related risks are rapidly evolving, as is the case for permafrost and glacial risks, an effective adaptation strategy would be to institute active monitoring of such risks. Finally, there are already a limited but growing number of cases where climate change is posing specific threats to humans and infrastructure. In such cases, there is a need for *niche* projects that proactively reduce such growing risks.

The following sections discuss these elements of this multi-pronged approach for dealing with the implications of climate change on natural hazards: harnessing existing natural hazard management frameworks and risk transfer mechanisms, making existing mechanisms more flexible and forward-looking, actively monitoring evolving climate risks, and implementing niche adaptation projects to address immediate hazards posed by climate change.

3. Harnessing existing mechanisms for natural hazards management and risk transfer

Alpine countries have always been exposed to the threats of natural hazards. In order to manage these phenomena, communities and authorities have used a variety of economic, legal and technical tools pertaining to different phase of the risk cycle (See Figure 11). Preparedness includes measures like early warning systems, the planning for rescue operations, evacuations, and temporary relocation. Prevention and protection measures contribute to limiting hazards exposure. These measures often offer different economic, social and environmental advantages and disadvantages. While protection can reduce exposure, it can also lead to complacency and reduce awareness, and can increase exposure by fostering the development of protected areas. On the other hand, spatial planning seeks to reduce damages by managing or limiting exposure. However, the long-term benefits of spatial planning often conflict with short term local economic interests as it reduces land-use opportunities. In addition, great precision in delineating risk areas is required as the risk exposure can vary considerably over short distances and living space in mountain region is very limited. Hence, efficient management of exposure through spatial planning may be politically hard to implement. Offsetting the financial burden through insurance schemes is also a key component of hazards management as it increases resilience of communities. But the large and often correlated damages combined with the lack of readily available information about hazards exposure can be problematic and reduce insurability.

3.1. National natural hazards management frameworks

Natural hazards management frameworks of Alpine countries offer various similarities but also differ according to their governance structure, the involvement of stakeholders in hazards management, and the scope and effectiveness of policies in place. This section briefly reviews these frameworks, outlining some of their strengths and weaknesses.

Figure 11. **The risk cycle**

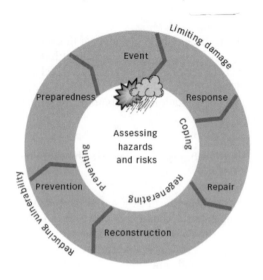

Source: ARE, 2006.

3.1.1. Austria

In Austria, natural hazards management responsibilities are shared between Federal, *Lander* and local authorities. In practice, the tasks of spatial planning, intervention and crisis management, as well as recovery measures fall under the responsibility of Lander and local authorities. At the federal level, the Austrian government provides guidance, expertise, as well as planning and funding resources for various hazards management activities. Among others, the Federal Ministry for Agriculture, Forestry, Environment and Water Management and its subordinated agencies play a leading role in natural hazards management.

The Federal Forest Engineering Service for Torrent and Avalanche Control (WLV) is responsible for planning and implementing technical and biological control/protection measures, while the Federal Water Engineering Authority (BWV) also contributes in establishing flood control and protection measures. These measures are financed by local governments and by the Disaster Relief Fund which falls under the responsibility of the Federal Ministry of Finance. The Disaster Relief Fund invests about EUR 150 million each year in preventive measures[19].

Hazards maps are developed by federal agencies, i.e. the WLV and BWV, in cooperation with local authorities and the community. As of 2005, hazards maps were

---

[19]   Elisabeth Ottawa, Austrian Federal Ministry of Finance (Bundesministerium für Finanzen), personal communication.

available for between 30 to 100% of areas at risk, depending on Landers. Complete coverage should be available by 2010 (BMLFUW, 2005). These hazards maps are not legally binding. Spatial planning legislations are provided by Landers and are generally limited to non-binding recommendations to local authorities. In implementing these recommendations, local authorities have, however, often prioritised the attractiveness of their community leading to planning deficiencies (BMLFUW, 2004). In fact, the BMLFUW (2004) states that "[t]o a considerable degree, the huge scale of damage [related to the 2002 floods] in many areas can be attributed to the missing legal connection between risk zone planning and regional planning" (p.396). In 2006, some Landers have strengthened their spatial planning policies to improve the management of natural hazards exposure. The Lander of Lower Austria simply banned construction in the areas within the reach of 100 year return period events from being considered as building land. At the same time, the Lander of Tyrol modified its spatial planning law to reduce its vagueness and define more precisely the criteria to be used to determine building land and endangered areas, thus reducing the flexibility of local authorities[20].

3.1.2. France

In France, the management of natural hazards is centralised and mainly controlled by the State. The Ministry of Ecology and Sustainable Development (MEDD) and, to a lesser extent, the Ministry of the Interior (MISILL) are involved in natural hazards management. At the local level, main actors in charge of natural hazard management are the *préfet,* representing the national government, and the mayors. Within the MEDD, the Direction for Pollution and Risk Prevention (DPPR) is in charge of establishing natural hazards prevention policies, while prevention measures are planned and implemented at the local level. Mayors have the responsibility of providing precautionary measures. Expertise and technical support is available from public agencies at the national level (*e.g.*, MeteoFrance, Cemagref) and departmental level (*e.g.*, Unit for Analysis of Risks and Preventive Information [CARIP]).

It is important to note that in France the prevention measures are centralised within one policy measure - the risk prevention plan (PPR), which was introduced in 1995. PPRs are adapted for each commune and must be developed and approved by the *préfet* in consultation with local authorities and representatives from the civil society (*e.g.*, Insurance, NGOs). PPRs provide information through the identification of hazard prone zones and also define the prevention measures to be undertaken by local authorities as well as potential uses for land and existing buildings within these zones. A national fund (Fond Barnier) also supports the implementation of PPRs through various measures (See Table 7).

---

[20]   Elisabeth Stix, Austrian Spatial Planning Conference (ÖROK), personal communication.

Table 7. **Activities funded by the Fond Barnier between 2003 and 2005, and projections until 2007**

Expenses (EUR million)	2003	2004	2005	2006*	2007*
Expropriations	3.05	1.71	7.98	0.66	0.28
Funding of PPR development	8.39	3.47	6.96	16.00	16.00
Prevention measures and temporary evacuation	0.01	0.04	14.92	7.10	7.10
Local studies and planning	-	-	6.36	30.00	30.00
Extraordinary measures	5.6	-	-	2.00	5.00
TOTAL	17.05	5.22	36.22	57.76	58.38

*Projections.
Source: MEDD/DPPR.

As of December 2005, more then 5000 communes had established a PPR. However, within Alpine regions[21] only 35% of the 2193 communes exposed to natural hazards had either a prescribed or approved PPR, outlining the need to further support and speed up the development of prevention efforts. Most of the prevention plans of Alpine communes are covering floods (92%) followed by mass movements (56%), avalanches (26%) and forest fires (14%) (See Appendix 6). It is also important to note that the non-respect of measures prescribed by PPRs can have legal consequences, hence providing a strong legal base for implementation of prevention measures. However, the lack of political will and the difficulties in establishing efficient cooperation between government levels undermines the hazard prevention efforts of the French government (OECD, 2006).

3.1.3. Switzerland

In Switzerland, the federal government provides the legal framework for natural hazards management as well as financial and technical support, while cantonal and local authorities are in charge at the operational level. The Federal Constitution as well as the federal forestry, river and engineering, and spatial planning laws provide the main legislation base for natural hazards management. The Federal Department of the Environment, Transport, Energy and Communication (DETEC) hosts the Federal Office for the Environment (FOEN) and the Federal Office for Civil protection (FOCP), which are the principal units in charge of natural hazard management. At the operational level most responsibilities related to natural hazards management lie with cantonal and communal authorities. The federal Forest Law stipulates that cantonal authorities must provide integrated natural hazards management by accounting for the interests of forest management, hydraulic building, protection of nature and landscape, agriculture, and

---

[21] French Alps were defined as the following departments: Alpes-de-Haute-Provence, Hautes-Alpes, Alpes Maritimes, Drôme, Isère, Savoie, Haute-Savoie, Var, and Vaucluse.

land-use planning. Cantons must also ensure security against natural hazards while using, to the extent possible, environmentally friendly measures.

Technical and biological protection measures are planned and implemented by local and cantonal authorities in conjunction with landowners and engineers. Federal authorities also participate in the process through subsidies which are made available to support protection efforts and may cover up to 50% of the costs. However, prevention measures related to single assets are the responsibility of the owner which may be a private party or a public institution.

The federal Forest Law stipulates that cantonal authorities must provide the documents necessary for protection against natural hazards. In Switzerland, the digital database StorMe, containing information on hazard events, is maintained and made available to cantonal authorities since the late 1990s so as to improve information and experience sharing. The central documents are hazards maps which delineate the high, medium, and low risk zones. These must be taken into account by authorities when developing land-use planning measures and regulations. Within high risk zones (red zones), new construction is usually prohibited while special construction constraints are imposed over the medium risk zones (blue zones). In the low risk zones (yellow zones) only sensitive buildings such as schools are prohibited. Actually, hazard maps coverage level in Switzerland reaches 66% for avalanches, 30% for floods, 29% for rockfalls and 23% for landslides (DETEC, 2006a). Complete coverage is expected by 2011. These documents are legally binding, which strengthens spatial planning laws by ensuring a more efficient implementation. In areas where either the population or substantial asset values are at risk from natural hazards, warning systems must be put in place by local authorities. To perform this task, local authorities are supported by national institutions such as the Swiss Meteorological Institute, and the Swiss federal Institute for Snow and Avalanche Research.

3.2.   *Insurance and risk transfer mechanisms*

Insurance mechanisms represent a key tool in spreading risk and mitigating the financial impact of natural hazards. Such mechanisms play a key role in increasing resilience to climate variability and change. Insurers can also contribute in transferring prevention incentives, through implementation of building codes or by defining insurance conditions based on risk exposure. In Austria, France and Switzerland, property insurance for natural hazards is generally available and therefore increases the resilience of these societies to climate change impacts. In addition, the EU has put in place the European Solidarity Fund to increase cross-border solidarity in facing disaster damages (see Box 5). However, increasing damages could threaten the insurability of natural hazards. Insurers have therefore sought to increase their efficiency and improve the transfer of prevention incentives in order to reduce the burden on the risk transfer schemes.

3.2.1. Austria

In Austria, insurance for natural hazards is offered by private insurers within an unregulated market. The insurance against natural hazards, including storms, snow pressure, rockfalls, and landslides, is available as an extended coverage above regular property insurance and is offered without deductible (full coverage). Premiums are based on expected aggregated damages but there is no spatial differentiation based on risk exposure. Since 1995, flood insurance can be bought separately, but only limited coverage is available, about EUR 3 500 to 5 000, and premiums are high. Extended coverage against flood damages can also be bought in areas which are expected to be unaffected by floods with return period of 100 years. As a result, flood coverage remains limited and expensive.[22]

Box 5. The European Union Solidarity Fund

The European Union Solidarity Fund (EUSF) was established in 2002 as a response to extreme flood events and related damages that occurred in the summer of that year. It does provide financial assistance in case of disaster resulting in national damages representing either over EUR 3 billion (2002 prices) or more than 0.6% of the gross national income. Exceptions to this rule can be made if a large share of a region's population is affected and its economic stability is threatened. The annual budget of the EU Solidarity Fund is of EUR 1 billion. The Fund can be used to cover expenses related to temporary accommodation, immediate and provisional repair of critical infrastructures (water, energy, transport), and cleaning-up of affected areas. For example, Austria received from the EUSF EUR 134 million for the 2002 flood and EUR 14.8 million for the 2005 flood[23]

Source: CEC, 2005.

A major obstacle encountered by the Austrian private insurance sector in offering flood insurance is the intervention of public authorities in compensating damages through the Austrian Disaster Fund, which reduces individual incentives to buy insurance. The public sector plays an active role in compensating natural hazards damages. Usually, these compensations only cover between 20-30 % of private losses (BMF 2006). They are financed by the Austrian federal (60%) and Landers (40%) governments. Under special occasions, compensation level can be higher, following the flood of 2002, compensation from one Lander to the next varied from 30% to 67% (Prettenthaler and Vetters, 2006).

---

[22] Gerahrd Wagner, UNIQA Versicherungen AG, personal communication.

[23] Elisabeth Ottawa, Austrian Ministry of Finance, personal communication.

3.2.2. France

In France, damages related to storms, hail, and snow, (SHS) are covered by the private insurance sector within a regulated market. On the other hand, damages caused by other hazards such as floods, avalanches, and land slides, are deemed to be non-insurable and are therefore covered by a public-private program (CatNat) supported by a public reinsurer, the Caisse Centrale de Réassurance (CCR). Legislation in place ensures the funding of the CatNat program through a surcharge or extra premium on property insurance across the whole country. This surcharge of 12%[24] is uniform across all regions and independent of natural hazards exposure. Property insurance being mandatory within France leads to a large diversification of risks as every property unit must participate in the program. The French insurance program is also directly linked with the implementation of prevention measures. First, 2% of the premium surcharge is diverted to the *fond Barnier* which funds prevention efforts undertaken by local authorities or individuals. The absence of an approved risk prevention plan within a commune can also lead to an increase in deductible. These linkages tend to reduce moral hazards[25], but with a mitigated success (Dumas *et al.*, 2005).

3.2.3. Switzerland

In Switzerland, public insurers, cantonal insurance monopolies (CIMs), offer unlimited natural hazards property protection in 19 cantons. The other seven cantons rely on regulated private insurance markets. In cantons covered by CIMs, natural hazards insurance is mandatory and in most of these cantons, premiums are uniform, and unrelated to natural hazards exposure. An interesting feature of the CIMs is their implication in organising and financing prevention activities. Their monopoly situation allows them to internalise the value of prevention efforts as it translates in lower damages and claims, and to perform an integrated management of hazards (Kamber, 2006, Ungern-Sternberg, 2004). CIMs can impose building codes and prescriptions for new construction in hazard prone areas[26] to reduce damage potential. In cases where building prescriptions do not reduce damage potential sufficiently, premium surcharges may also be imposed by CIMs[27].

Seven cantons of Switzerland rely on regulated private insurance and many of them are located in Alpine regions, including the cantons of Valais, Ticino and Geneva. Unlike CMIs, insurance coverage offered by private insurers is limited. Although

---

[24] Premium surcharge is 12% with one exception for motor vehicles for which the surcharge is 6%.

[25] The term moral hazard is used to define a situation created by asymmetric information and in which the presence of insurance or risk transfer schemes leads policyholders to accept greater risk exposure.

[26] Building code and prescriptions are enforced mainly in blue zones (medium risk) while new construction is forbidden in red zones (high risk).

[27] Markus Fisher, GVA Graubünden, personal communication.

insurance is not mandatory in all seven cantons, 95% of buildings are actually insured. Insurance premiums are regulated and are uniform across all regions, and, therefore, do not take into account the risk exposure of particular buildings. Deductibles and coverage level are also uniform across regions and independent of risk exposure.[28]

3.3. Assessment of existing mechanisms

From a global perspective the Alpine countries clearly have a very high adaptive capacity with regard to dealing with natural hazards. Institutional structures and regulations for managing natural hazards are in place, as are insurance mechanisms to facilitate risk transfer. While early hazard mitigation efforts focused primarily on disaster recovery, there has been growing emphasis on disaster prevention in the Alpine countries. These measures are broadly synergistic with anticipatory adaptation. Another positive trend has been the growing emphasis on integrated natural hazards management that emphasises stakeholders' involvement and awareness as well as attention to all elements of the risk cycle (from prevention to recovery). This has translated in an increased coordination and cooperation of parties involved in natural hazards management and a greater emphasis on prevention measures that had been little used in the past. Box 6 presents two relevant initiatives undertaken by the Alpine Convention and at the national level in Switzerland. The movement towards integration management led to the strengthening of spatial planning laws and the development of a greater information base including hazards maps to support prevention efforts and raise awareness. Integrated hazard management has many advantages and can significantly improve the capacity to adapt by increasing the efficiency of actual institutions and by improving co-operation and awareness. It also offers several obvious entry-points for factoring in climate risk information, for example in hazard mapping, spatial planning, as well as the design of prevention measures.

However, this assessment also demonstrates that countries in the Alpine arc nevertheless face significant challenges in dealing with current hazards, let alone the implications of climate change. For example, integrated management schemes are not yet fully operational in Alpine countries, and in many cases implementation remains difficult. In France, natural hazards prevention is still suffering from a lack of public interest in hazards knowledge and culture, weak prevention efforts due to moral hazards problems, and difficulties in establishing efficient cooperation between public actors (OECD, 2006). In Austria, a review of the risk transfer scheme in 2003 concluded that "insufficient awareness is often coupled with data insufficiencies; moreover, past efforts have often been restricted to technical protective measures. Integrated adaptive strategies comprising a package of technical, spatial planning, organizational, economic and climate and education policy measures are rare exceptions" (Hyll et al., 2003). Switzerland is likely the most advanced country of the Alpine arc in terms of integrated management of natural hazards. However, as of 2004, the implementation was only partial (PLANAT, 2004).

---

[28] Max Gretener, Swiss Insurance Association, personal communication.

Box 6. **Development of integrated management strategies**

Platform on Natural Hazards – Alpine Convention (PLANALP)

In 2004, the Alpine Convention established the *Platform on Natural Hazards - Alpine Convention (PLANALP).* The goal of PLANALP is to develop common natural hazards management strategies among the Alpine Convention members (Austria, Germany, France, Italy, Liechtenstein, Monaco, Slovenia, Switzerland) and appropriate adaptation strategies in response to changing conditions, in particular to climatic changes and their impacts on mountain regions. The first work program of PLANALP was established in spring 2006 and includes identifying "best practices", fostering cross-border exchange of experience, strengthening risk dialogue in particular with the public, and increasing cooperation among Alpine Convention parties in order to foster an integrated and common natural risk management. The initial activities of PLANALP are taking place within the EU INTERREG IIIB programme on "Alpine Space". The need for integrated natural hazards management was further supported by the Declaration of the IXth Alpine Conference on Climate Change in the Alps.

Source: Alpine Convention, 2006a; Alpine Convention, 2006b; Alpine Convention, 2006c.

National Platform for Natural Hazards – Switzerland (PLANAT)

In 1997, the Swiss Federal Council created the National Platform for Natural Hazards (PLANAT). The mandate of this interdisciplinary commission was to 1) develop a new hazards management strategy, 2) induce a cultural shift in natural hazards management approach - 'from protection against dangers to risk management", and 3) to coordinate actions to foster experience and knowledge sharing at the national and international level. In developing this strategy, the role of climate change in exacerbating risks related to natural hazards was acknowledged.

The PLANAT strategy, presented in November 2004, is based on an integrated risk management approach. It seeks to integrate all stages of the risk cycle and other risks such as technological hazards. Other aspects of the strategy are the raising of risk awareness, the integration of the different stakeholders in hazards management, and the acceptance of residual risk by these stakeholders. A sustainable approach is also fostered by including economic, environmental and social aspects in selecting appropriate natural hazards management measures. Finally, the PLANAT strategy represents a long-term and forward looking approach as it aims to prevent the development of new sources of risk and recommends frequent reassessment of risk (every five years).

Source: PLANAT, 2004.

Additionally, some key features of natural hazards management are deficient in some countries. For example, flood insurance coverage is still very limited in Austria. While government compensations have been providing some relief to individuals, coverage remains limited (usually 20 to 30 %). In addition, recent government intervention, in addition to being costly for governments, has been reducing private insurance ability to offer extended and affordable coverage (Hyll *et al.,* 2003). On the other hand, France is offering a good insurance coverage to private property owners. Given the availability and affordability of coverage, the weakness of the French system is the lack of effective prevention policies which leads to problems of moral hazards (Dumas *et al.,* 2005, OECD, 2006). Spatial planning deficiencies have also been recently observed in Austria due to the lax regulation in place in most Landers (BMLFUW, 2004). Switzerland, meanwhile, appears to be faring relatively well, demonstrating stronger spatial planning laws and comprehensive insurance coverage, although the cost of insurance has been increasing over the last decades in many "Alpine" cantons.

It is also noteworthy that, in all countries surveyed, there appears to be very little use of economic incentives to support and strengthen actual hazard prevention efforts. Insurance premiums, for example, are generally not linked to risk exposure, thereby reducing the incentives for undertaking risk prevention. There are, however, some exceptions. For example, in some cantons of Switzerland, CIMs can increase premiums in areas at risk (as defined by hazards maps) if the implementation of building codes and restrictions does not reduce risk exposure sufficiently. However, the scope of this tool is limited as the premium increases are modest and seldom implemented[29]. Another example can be observed in France. Since 2000, the deductibles of the CatNat insurance can be increased in a commune if "CatNat events" have occurred after 1995 and still no PPR has been prescribed or approved (see Appendix 7). However, despite a significant increase in the number of PPR prescribed or approved since 2000, the fairness of such policy with respect to individuals is questionable (Dumas *et al.,* 2005) and the effectiveness of PPRs as a prevention measure is also limited (OECD, 2006).

One reason why insurance premiums have generally not been linked to local risk exposure is the inability of the many insurers to undertake hazard risk assessment. Another, perhaps more important, reason is the solidarity principle which goes against penalising those at greater risk. However, given the increasing availability of hazard information, the social benefit of solidarity may need to be weighed against the positive incentives created by risk based insurance for individuals and communities to undertake prevention efforts.

4.   Enhancing the robustness and flexibility of natural hazards management

While the strengthening and efficient implementation of existing mechanisms for natural hazards management would constitute a strong basis for climate change adaptation, that alone would not be enough. This is because natural hazards management relies on information that is *retrospective* in terms of where particular hazards occur, how often, and with what intensity. However, all three parameters –

---

[29]   Markus Fisher, GVA Graubunden, personal communication.

location/spatial coverage, frequency, and intensity – can change, in some cases quite dramatically, as climate change impacts manifest themselves. This for example is particularly the case for glacial hazards, debris flows, and mass movements which are quite sensitive to rising temperatures and changes in precipitation. In other words, the past – which forms the basis of current natural hazards management practices – might no longer be a good basis for managing hazards under climate change.

How can natural hazards management practices be more *prospective*, given the significant uncertainties associated with the evolution of many climate change related hazards? One strategy might be to raise the precautionary standard for hazards management to factor in the changes in hazard frequency/intensity. Including more intense and extreme events into the planning process should lead to more robust measures. For example, in Switzerland hazards maps have been adjusted to include events with 300 years return period instead of being limited to 100 year events. Adjustments also took place in the planning of emergency measures which now account for events with 1 000 years return period.[30] Whether climate change is considered or not, raising the precautionary standards increases the resilience to more frequent/intense extremes.

Another strategy that can be adopted is to build in more frequent updating of hazard maps, which serve as the basis for spatial planning, insurance conditions and other response measures. Frequent updating of such maps could enable them to take into account evolving hazard profiles, as is particularly the case for permafrost and glacier related hazards. In the three countries surveyed, the criteria used to trigger a review of hazard exposure and maps are sometimes vague and in all cases reactive in nature. In the case of Switzerland the policies regarding the updating of hazard maps are fairly vague, calling only for "periodic renewal". In France, the review of PPRs and hazard maps is only required if the existing risk assessments are put in doubt by new events. Similarly, in the case of Austria renewal of flood risk maps is called for only if there are "changes in the conditions in a catchment or if there are new findings as a result of disasters". The updating of flood hazard maps in Austria has been rather uneven. While some hazard maps, approved in 2000 or 2001, have already been reviewed, this is not the case for many others that were developed much earlier (between 1985-1998) (BMLFUW, 2005b). In addition to frequent updates that take into account recent events, another possibility would be to also include information on *anticipated* risks posed by climate change within hazards maps. For example, the proposed Flood Directive of the Commission of the European Communities requires that climate change information be included in flood risk assessments underpinning the development of flood maps and flood management plans (see Box 7).

---

[30] Roberto Loat, Federal Office for the Environment, personal communication.

Box 7. **The development of a European flood directive**

Following the large human and economic damages imposed by flood events in several European countries between 1998 and 2004, the Commission of the European Communities (CEC) identified flood damages as being an issue that required Community level action due to the potential exacerbation of damages by climate change impacts on the scale and frequency of floods and the increasing vulnerability of people and assets. The CEC then developed a proposal for a Flood Directive aiming at the reduction and management of flood impact on human health, properties and the environment. The Flood Directive is expected to complement the EU Disaster Fund by offering an alternative to reactive emergency measures financed by this fund. It also complements the Water Framework Directive (WFD) adopted in 2000 which displays synergies with climate change adaptation by providing sustainable and forward-looking integrated river basin water management plans, but does not address climate change directly.

The proposed Flood Directive is based on three important steps. The first step is to perform an assessment of flood risk which shall include "an assessment of the likelihood of future floods based on hydrological data, types of floods and the projected impact of climate change and land use trends" (CEC, 2006 p.14). Following this assessment, flood hazard maps are to be produced and a risk management plan to be developed by 2015. It also aims at including all aspects of the risk cycle with a particular focus on prevention, protection and preparedness; and establishing the appropriate protection level to reduce environmental, human and economic risks. The entire process is expected to be repeated every six years in order to incorporate new information. However, the challenge of mainstreaming uncertain climate change information within current decision making processes is not addressed by the proposed directive, as it does not provide details on how information on climate change impacts would actually be taken into account within the implementation of flood risk management plan.

Source: CEC, 2006.

The need for more frequent updating of hazard maps however must be carefully balanced against the significant costs associated with their production. Costs of flood hazard maps in Austria, for example, range from less than EUR 1 000 to over EUR 20 000 per kilometre of river covered (BMLFUW, 2005b). Beyond the issue of costs, it is also important to note that hazard maps in turn serve as the basis for spatial planning and regulations, and there might be significant transaction costs (and even legal challenges) if significant changes are made to such maps on a frequent basis, that too on the basis of model based scenarios. A mid-way solution, however, might be to use hazard maps that incorporate scenarios of future impacts as advisory, and not regulatory, tools. For example, such maps could be beneficial in raising awareness and by making climate change information available to decision makers. Based on such information decision-makers may also display greater caution in implementing long-term and irreversible investment projects in areas that might be at high risk in the future.

Much like public decision-makers, the insurance companies too largely rely on retrospective information. So far, approaches used by insurers within the Alpine Arc do not factor in the impact of climate change. Going from a pricing methodology based on past evidence to the inclusion of theoretical considerations surrounded by large uncertainties may prove to be difficult to accept for consumers, and to implement by insurers, especially within a competitive insurance sector (Loster, 2005). The climate change awareness of Alpine insurers is growing, but they are only starting to take action to be better prepared to face these changes. In Austria, private insurers are funding the development of local climate change scenarios in order to improve climate change information[31]. While in France, the MRN (Mission des sociétés d'assurances pour la connaissance et la prévention des Risques Naturels) is slowly exploring the consequence of climate change on insurance reserves and pricing but as yet no real approach or framework has been developed[32]. Although challenging, adaptation of insurance products to include climate change information would contribute to raising awareness and diffusing adaptation incentives within communities.

5.   Responses to observed climate change impacts

In some areas, the climate change signal may justify measures more directly focused on addressing climate change impacts. In these cases, synergies with other objectives should be exploited to the extent possible and flexibility should also remain a key criterion in a dynamic setting such as climate change. The increasing incidence of glacier and permafrost related hazards is the clearest signal of climate change impacts on natural hazards in Alpine regions. Trends in permafrost melt and glacier retreat as well as natural hazards related to these changes have been observed for many years now. To maintain hazards protection levels, the impacts of these trends should therefore be included in the management of hazard in periglacial areas. Within the European Alps, various efforts have taken place in this sense. Starting with national and supranational efforts to document these trends and potential impacts on periglacial natural hazards, but also to develop tools to facilitate the integration of this information into the decision making processes and the assessment of potential adaptation measures. Despite the clear climate change signals, only very few local examples exist where concrete measures have been implemented.

5.1.   Regional and national responses

5.1.1. GLACIORISK

The GLACIORISK research project took place over the 2001-2003 period and looked at glacier catastrophes in Europe. The specific objectives of the project were to

---

[31]   Gerhard Wagner, UNIQA Versicherungen AG, and Thomas Hlatky, Grazer Wechselseitige Versicherung, personal communication.

[32]   Roland Nussbaum, Mission des sociétés d'assurances pour la connaissance et la prévention des Risques Naturels, personal communication.

detect, survey, and prevent glacial disasters in order to better assess the risk potential under changing climatic and socio-economic conditions. In order to do so, the project spanned and integrated the work from experts across the entire Alpine arc. Various work packages were established, each taking place within various institutions and countries, *e.g.*, Cemagref (France), Swiss Federal Institute of Technology Zurich, University of Salzburg (Austria), Societa Meteorologica Subalpina (Italy). The work packages of the project integrated most steps leading to climate change adaptation, from data collection to economic analysis and decision aids.

In a first step, the project provided information on glacier and hazards events through a database which gave access to past experiences across all regions. The study focused on events related to GLOFs, glacier stability, avalanches related to serac falls, and changes in glacier length. The project aimed at raising awareness of glacial risk through the dissemination of information to the general public and end users. Different atlases of glaciers posing higher risks were published for various countries, in addition to the realisation of a video on glacial risks.

The different glacial hazards were also investigated by scientists to increase our understanding of phenomena, and improve the prediction and mitigation capacity of these hazards. The research included the gathering of existing worldwide knowledge and field experiments in the Alps. Numerical simulations of glacier and hazards were performed to improve the understanding of triggering conditions, magnitude and occurrence of events, examine climate change sensitivity and increase predictability of events. The ultimate aim of this exercise was to perform hazards zoning and produce hazard maps. However, the current lack of knowledge about the various processes driving the incidence of these hazards, *e.g.*, the sub-glacial hydrological systems, prevented the research team from producing hazards maps. Nevertheless, risk assessment guidelines have emerged for the project. Guidelines include the development of hazards scenarios, potential damage estimates and inventory of prevention measures which are then presented to stakeholders in a risk assessment workshop. A second workshop is then carried out with decision-makers and hazards experts to evaluate prevention measures.

As part of this process, a risk analysis framework was developed in order to make this information as useful as possible for decision makers, and to allow for the evaluation of measures while accounting for various scenarios and societal risk perception. Based on cost effectiveness, the results account for climate change information and societal perception of risk, and allow decision maker to prioritise responses accordingly (See Figures 12 and 13). For the canton of Valais, Switzerland, the cost-effectiveness results highlight the advantage of monitoring and prediction strategies relative to more costly infrastructure such as drainage tunnels and road and railways protections.

Figure 12. **Annual costs and risk reduction of different adaptation measures in canton of Valais, Switzerland**

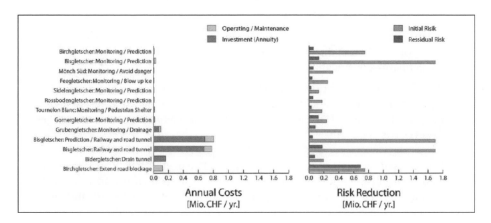

Source: Richard and Gay (2003), and Charly Wuilloud, Forestry Services, Valais, Switzerland.

Figure 13. **Cost effectiveness of adaptation measures for glacier hazards in Canton of Valais, Switzerland**

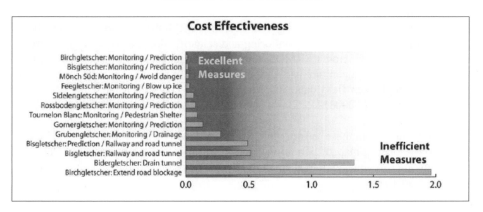

Source: Richard and Gay (2003), and Charly Wuilloud, Forestry Services, Valais, Switzerland.

5.1.2. *The EU Permafrost and Climate in Europe (PACE) project*

The PACE project is another example of cross-border research on climate change impacts on Alpine environment and natural hazards. The PACE project started in 1997 with three distinct objectives:

- to establish a framework for monitoring the impact of global climate change on permafrost geothermal regimes in the mountains of Europe;

- to develop methods of mapping and modelling the distribution of thermally sensitive mountain permafrost, and predicting changes in this distribution resulting from climate change;

- to provide new, process-based, methods for assessing environmental and geotechnical hazards associated with mountain permafrost degradation.

The research program provided insightful information on permafrost evolution in the European mountains. Data obtained from the monitoring network, result suggest a warming trend of permafrost, but also large interannual fluctuation of due to changes in snow cover (Harris *et al.*, 2003).

Then, based on topographic, climatic and soil characteristics, the research group established a protocol to identify potential impacts of permafrost melt on natural hazards. In a first step, the protocol suggests identifying potential hazards through site reconnaissance and analysis of data from geo-climatic and historical events. In a second step, detailed permafrost mapping is suggested, which requires further investigation through geophysical surveys and borehole drilling.

5.1.3. National measures in Switzerland

Switzerland took part in the PACE and GLACIORISK projects but also developed the Permafrost Monitoring Switzerland (PERMOS) network which has been established to provide long-term monitoring and scientific documentation of permafrost evolution in the Swiss Alps. PERMOS activities include collection of data concerning snow cover, ground temperature and various boreholes in permafrost areas. In addition, air photos complement field data, to provide a more comprehensive view of spatial changes. (Mühll *et al.*, 2004).

Building upon these efforts the Swiss Federal Office for the Environment recently developed a map of permafrost in Switzerland, which was made available to cantons in order to be taken into account in hazards maps and spatial planning activities (DETEC, 2006b).

5.2. Local adaptation measures

Threats stemming from periglacial hazards are quite localised in nature and therefore concrete adaptation measures are undertaken at the local level. Some local communities have been awakened to potential climate change impacts on natural hazards through scientific discoveries and ongoing hazards events. In response, these communities have sought to address these risks as efficiently as possible, by adopting synergistic and flexible adaptation measures.

5.2.1. Responses to the increasing glacial risks in Macugnaga

The Monte Rosa is one of the highest summits of the Alps, located in the Pennine Alps, and extending from Switzerland to the Italian region of Piedmont. Within the Monte Rosa massif, recent glacier instability has threatened the mountain village of Macugnaga, located at 1 327 m altitude, in the Verbano-Cusio-Ossola Province. The town is located at the base of Monte Rosa, and is know for its mine (Miniera della Guia), but as in many other Alpine villages, the main economic activity of the town is tourism due to the opportunities for skiing in winter, and hiking in summer.

The problematic situation came from the Belvedere glacier, located on the east face of the Monte Rosa. The glacier generated 7 lake outbursts within the last century. However, in 2001 signs of glacier instability were found. The glacier started a surge-type movement leading to intensification of rockfalls and the formation of a glacial lake in 2002 (see Figure 14). Rockfalls and icefalls mainly threatened the tourism areas, *e.g.*, ski runs and hiking trails, while large ice falls and lake outburst also threatened settlements in the valley. These hazards threats created security problems which also translated directly into economic problems due to the closing of an important ski run.

Figure 14. **Belvedere Glacier and its glacial lakes**

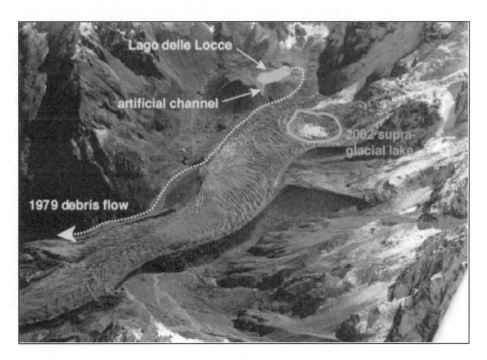

Photo: C. Rothenbühler, Academia Engiadina, Samedan, Switzerland.

These surge type movements are quite atypical for the Belvedere glacier. While not being necessarily linked to climate change, the movement is likely a result of alteration in the glacier systems caused by changes in boundary conditions (*e.g.*, soil and air temperature). Ice avalanche and rockfalls are natural for a glacier but can increase in frequency during glacier transition periods, which may be induced by climate change.

On the other hand, the formation of the lake at the Belvedere Glacier was directly linked to warm periods. There is evidence that the conditions in Monte Rosa and the Belvedere Glacier are undergoing rapid change. For glacier hazards, times of transition are most problematic and hazards frequency and magnitude will likely evolve over time. The probabilities of lake formation will likely increase in some areas, while in others areas there will be an increase in rockfalls due to glacier retreat. However, the evolution and timing of hazards remain uncertain[33].

Upon observation of glacier instability in 2001, local authorities were alerted. Monitoring of the situation was undertaken by local mountain guides and since the situation evolved quite rapidly, a crisis committee was formed to manage the situation and ensure public safety. The committee was formed by the National Civil Protection of Italy and included various experts (*e.g.*, geologist, engineers).

As a response, and given the uncertainty of future hazards developments, the decision was taken to implement a monitoring strategy in combination with flexible protection measures. This decision was guided by meetings between the regional civil protection authorities and a scientific committee, which provided a priority list based on the frequency and magnitude of potential events, as well as the possibility of chain events. These monitoring measures were implemented starting in 2001 and included:

- field measurements (1-2 times a year);

- aerial photos (2-3 times a year);

- automatic cameras, videos;

- automatic instruments to take various measurements, such as ice thickness, pressure, lake formation.[34]

As well, in order to maintain ski operations, some excavation work was performed and walls were erected to protect skiers against rocks and ice avalanches. In 2003, following the increasing lake volume, a high voltage cable and a pump were installed to empty the lake. Computer models and hazards scenarios were also used to assess flood dangers for citizens leading to the partial evacuation of the village. In the aftermath of these events, risk mapping and spatial planning measures were also complemented by local authorities.[27]

---

[33] Andreas Kääb, University of Oslo, personal communication.

[34] Paolo Semino, Direzione Opere Pubbliche, Region Piemonte, personal communication.

5.2.2. Dams for avalanche and debris flow protection in Pontresina

The town of Pontresina, a small traditional village of 1 847 inhabitants in the southeast of Switzerland, is a pioneer in responding to climatic change. The town is located within the Engadine region at 1800 meters above sea level and is well known for tourism activities. Beside the historic value of the town which has buildings dating from the 13th century, Pontresina's economy is centred on the tourism activities that it offers, including 350 km of ski runs during winter and 500 km of hiking trails during summer, and resulting in the accommodation of more than 90 000 visitors per year.

Being located at the foot of the Schafberg Mountain which is famous for avalanches, the village of Pontresina has a long history in dealing with natural hazards. In fact, the town was originally built in two separate parts in order to limit potential avalanche damages since the central part served as a channel for avalanches. But the expansion of the town led to the development of the central part of the city, thus increasing the exposure to avalanche threats. In response, starting in the 1970's the community erected 16 km of protecting fences on the slopes of the Schafberg Mountain which contribute to protection against avalanches and rockfalls.

In addition, the mountain is partly covered by permafrost. The permafrost of the Schafberg Mountain is slowly thawing (Switzerland, 2005). In the early 1990s, permafrost was warming but the thin snow cover of the 1995 and 1996 winters stopped this trend. Since 1997, the temperature at depths of 10m has slowly increased again (Mühll et al. 2004). The slow thawing of the permafrost became problematic for inhabitants of Pontresina as it reduced slope stability and increased the material volume of potential debris flows. It is estimated that around 100 000 m³ of material could slide downwards and reach the town of Pontresina (SwissInfo, 2001). The phenomenon is also problematic for actual protection fences as these are anchored in permafrost. Protection fences have been observed to creep downhill by 5 to 20 cm per year since the late 1980s, which phenomenon may reduce their protective capacity and their durability (SwissInfo, 2003).

Both of the potential hazards, avalanches and mass movements, could impose significant damages to the town of Pontresina. Large debris flows can impose substantial damages and could also negatively affect the tourism industry. In response to these threats, the town council of Pontresina decided in 2001 to use the synergy between protection against avalanches and potential debris flows stemming from permafrost thawing to erect a dam which can protect the town against 280 000 m³ avalanches and 100 000 m³ debris flows (see Figure 16). The federal and cantonal governments funded 75% of the project which cost more than EUR 4.5 million (CHF 7 million) in total (Switzerland, 2005).

Figure 15. Dams for avalanche and debris flow protection in Pontresina

Photo: Markus Weidmann, Chur, Switzerland.

5.2.3. Modification of the Flaz river bed in Samedan

In the last decades, the Samedan community, located in Engadine, Switzerland, has experienced several floods due the overflow of the Flaz River. These events caused extensive damages and occurred in spite of dam constructions and land-use development restrictions imposed by the canton of Grisons. As a result, the local, cantonal and federal governments decided to improve the existing prevention measures as these measures were judged to be insufficient. The impact of glacier retreat and shift in the snowline induced by climatic change, both of which may affect flood risk, were taken into account in the risk assessment (Switzerland, 2005).

A first solution to this problem would have been a reinforcement of the existing dike and an increased canalisation of the river, thus bolstering existing protection measures. This is a common solution proposed to adapt prevention measures to extreme events and changes in terms of intensity and frequency of floods. But ultimately, the solution adopted contrasted with the traditional approach and relied to a greater extent on adaptation of land-use along the river bed. It was decided that the river should recover its natural bed over 4.2 km in order to get the Flaz River to recover a regime

 CLIMATE CHANGE IN THE EUROPEAN ALPS — ISBN 92-64-03168-5 — © OECD 2007

closer to its natural one (see Figure 16). The areas located on both sides of the river became buffer areas, absorbing part of the flooding waters. An adjacent airfield could also act as a buffer zone in case of flooding. The project included environmental concerns, as a side of the river was devoted to the conservation of the fauna and the flora. By this measure, the community also hopes to reap tourism benefits from a cross-country track.

Figure 16. **View of the permafrost areas on the Schafberg Mountain above Pontresina**

Photo: C. Rothenbühler, Academia Engiadina, Samedan, Switzerland.

This adaptation decision is the result of long consensus and extended negotiations between the local community, cantonal authorities, the Parliament and the federal authorities (FOEN), and different associations. The project is extensive, including the construction of six new bridges and the excavation of 300 000 m^3 of soil, for a total cost of about CHF 28 400 000 (EUR 18 325 000). The Confederation and Canton fund 75% of the cost, the remainder is funded by the community and some other partners.[35]

---

[35] Projekt Hochwasserschutz Samedan 2002 bis 2006, www.flaz.ch.

Figure 17. **Modification of the Flaz river bed**

Old river bed (Flaz)

River bed (Inn)

New river bed (Flaz)

Foto: C. Rothenbühler, 2003

Source: www.flaz.ch.

6. Discussion and policy implications

Natural hazards have significant impact on Alpine societies and economies, particularly floods and storms. Climate change is expected to increase the frequency and intensity of many of these hazards and shifts their spatial or temporal distribution. Hazards in glacial and permafrost areas have strong linkages to climate change. While their economic significance might be low from a national perspective they can, nevertheless, have strong impact on local economies. On the other hand, hazards which have considerably higher economic and social significance, such as floods and windstorms, have more complex and less certain linkages with climate change. However the uncertainty of climatic change impacts on floods and winter storms should not prevent adaptation from taken place although the nature of the response measure may be altered.

Climate change provides yet one more reason to improve the efficiency of existing natural hazards management activities. The institutional capacity of the Alpine countries included in this analysis is clearly very high. But many challenges remain in order to achieve an optimal hazards management policy. The implementation of land-use planning regulations remains difficult in many Alpine regions and there appears to be very little use of economic incentives to support and strengthen hazard prevention efforts. Insurance mechanisms represent an important tool through which market signals can encourage prevention and adaptation. Ensuring proper insurance coverage and exploiting the potential benefit of insurance markets represent a key opportunity for Alpine countries to foster risk awareness, prevention, and economic efficiency. Given the increasing availability of hazard information, the positive incentives created by risk-based insurance for individuals and communities to undertake prevention efforts may call for a reassessment.

While the lack of available information about past events often limits the efficiency of current hazard management, many resources are actually devoted to increase this information base and develop hazards maps. However, under constantly evolving conditions, forward-looking mechanism will also be required to take anticipated risks into account efficiently. The provision of high quality information on climate change impacts and of decision aids to help local authorities assess and quantify climate change risk will certainly be needed. However, even based on past evidence, natural hazards management decisions are often contentious as they restrain economic activity and impose significant cost (*e.g.*, expropriation, protection structure). Taking such decisions based on uncertain climate change scenarios will be even more contentious and politically hard to sustain. There might even be legal challenges to the inclusion of uncertain climate change information in hazard maps which serve as the basis for spatial planning, insurance conditions, and other response measures.

A key question, therefore, is how best to factor climate change information into the current legal and economic frameworks. Alternatives which can partly answer this question may also include raising the precautionary standard for hazards management, frequently updating hazard maps, and adopting more flexible frameworks. These are of specific importance when considering long-lived capital investments such as properties and infrastructures. However, these strategies are also costly as they too can limit land-use opportunities and require significant resources. The experience of Alpine countries also reinforce the idea that monitoring can be an efficient adaptation measures, especially in cases where climate related risks are observed and rapidly evolving as is the case for permafrost and glacier hazards. Also, despite the observed changes in hazards risk within glacier and permafrost areas, there are still a very limited number of adaptation projects which have actually been implemented. While not all areas may be at risk, these regions may require greater attention from policy-makers, and permanent monitoring frameworks might prove to be very helpful and efficient in managing such climate change risk.

References

Abegg, B. (1996), "Klimaänderung und Tourismus", Klimafolgenforschung am Beispiel des Wintertourismus in den Schweizer Alpen, Zurich.

Abegg, B. *et al.* (1997), "Climate Impact Assessment im Tourismus", *Die Erde*, Vol.128, pp. 105-116.

Amt für Seilbahnen (ed.) (2006), "Seilbahnen in Südtirol 2005", Autonome Provinz Bozen-Südtirol, Bozen/Bolzano, available in German and Italian at: http://www.provinz.bz.it/mobilitaet/3803/seilbahnen/seilbahnen%202005.pdf.

Allianz Umweltstiftung (ed.) (2005), "Gschwender Horn: Eine Schneise für die Natur", In: Allianz Journal April 2005, Munich, available at http://allianz-umweltstiftung.de.

Alpine Convention (2006a), "Déclaration de la IXe conférence Alpine sur les changements climatiques dans les Alpes ", Permanent Secretariat of the Alpine Convention, Innsbruck, Austria, Nopvember 2006.

Alpine Convention (2006b), "Working programme 2005 - 2006 Platform on Natural Hazards - Alpine Convention ", Permanent Secretariat of the Alpine Convention, Innsbruck, Austria, April 2006. Available at www.planat.ch.

Alpine Convention (2006c), "La Plate-forme Risques naturels de la Convention Alpine démarre son projet de travail". Press release, Permanent Secretariat of the Alpine Convention, Innsbruck, Austria, May 2006. Available at www.planat.ch.

ARE (2006), Recommendation – Spatial Planning and Natural Hazards, Swiss Office for Spatial Development, Berne, March 2006.

Association of British Insurers (2005), "Financial risks of climate change – Summary report", London, UK.

Bayerisches Landesamt für Umweltschutz: Information on snowmaking available at http://www.bayern.de/lfu/index.html.

Bathurst, J.C. *et al.* (2005), "Scenario modeling of basin-scale shallow landslide sediment yield, Valsassina, Italian Southern Alps", *Natural Hazards and Earth System Science*, Vol.5, pp. 189-202.

Behm, M., Raffeiner, G. and Schöner, W. (2006), Auswirkungen der Klima- und Gletscheränderung auf den Alpinismus. Umweltdachverband, Vienna.

Behringer, J., Bürki, R. and Fuhrer J. (2000), "Participatory integrated assessment of adaptation to climate change in Alpine tourism and mountain agriculture", *Integrated Assessment*, Vol.1, pp. 331-338.

Beniston, M. (1997), "Variations of snow depth and duration in the Swiss Alps over the last 50 years: links to changes in large-scale climatic forcings", *Climatic Change*, Vol.36, pp. 281-300.

Beniston, M. (2000), "Environmental Change in Mountains and Uplands", Arnold/Hodder and Stoughton/Chapman and Hall Publishers, London, UK, and Oxford University Press, New York, USA, 172 pp.

Beniston, M. (2003), "Climatic Change in Mountain Regions: a review of possible impacts", *Climatic Change*, Vol. 59, pp. 5-31.

Beniston, M. (2004), "Climatic change and its impacts. An overview focusing on Switzerland", Kluwer Academic Publishers, Dordrecht/The Netherlands and Boston/USA, 296 pp.

Beniston, M. (2005), "Mountain climates and climatic change: an overview of processes focusing on the European Alps", *Pure and Applied Geophysics*, Vol. 162, pp.1587-1606.

Beniston, M., (2006), "Climatic Change in the Alps: perspectives and impacts", OECD – Wengen 2006 workshop: Adaptation to the impacts of climate change in the European Alps, Wengen, Switzerland, October 4-6.

Beniston, M., Keller, F. and Goyette, S. (2003), "Snow pack in the Swiss Alps under changing climatic conditions: an empirical approach for climate impact studies", *Theoretical and Applied Climatology,* Vol.74, pp.19-31.

Beniston, M. *et al.* (2003), "Estimates of snow accumulation and volume in the Swiss Alps under changing climate conditions", *Theoretical and Applied Climatology,* Vol.76, pp. 125-140.

Bieger, T. and Laesser, C. (2005), Erfolgsfaktoren, Geschäfts- und Finanzierungsmodelle für eine Bergbahnindustrie im Wandel. St. Gall.

BMLFUW (Umweltbundesamt) (2004), "Environmental Situation in Austria", Seventh State of the Environment Report of the Federal Minister of Environment to the National Assembly of the Austrian Parliament, Vienna, September 2004.

BMLFUW (2005a), "Austrian Service for Torrent and Avalanche Control", Federal Ministry of Agriculture, Forestry, Environment and Water Management, Vienna, Austria.

BMLFUW (2005b), "Gefahrenzonenausweisung und Abflussuntersuchungen der Bundeswasserbauverwaltungen in Österreich", June 2005. Available at www.wassernet.at/filemanager/download/11305/.

Böhm, R. *et al.* (2001), "Regional temperature variability in the European Alps: 1760-1998 from homogenized instrumental time series", *International Journal of Climatology*, vol.(21), pp.1779-1801.

Breiling M. (1994a), "Climate variability: The impact on the national economy, the Alpine environments of Austria and the need for local action". Paper presented at Conference Snow and Climate, Geneva, September 1994.

Breiling M. (1994b), "Climate variability: the near term perspective of possible climate change and its impact on winter tourist industry and the Alpine environment". Lecture notes to Seminar Potsdam Institute for Climate Impact Research, Potsdam, January 1994.

Breiling M. (1998a), "Mountain Regions, Winter Tourism and Possible Climate Change: Example Austria". Symposium: Concern for Environment. Komaba Campus, University of Tokyo. June 1998.

Breiling M. (1998b), "The role of snow cover in Austrian economy during 1965 and 1995 and possible consequences under a situation of temperature change". Paper presented at Conference of Japanese Snow and Ice Society. Niigata, October 1998.

Breiling M. and Charamza P. (1999), "The impact of global warming on winter tourism and skiing: a regionalised model for Austrian snow conditions", *Regional Environmental Change* Vol. 1(1), pp.4-14.

Bürki, R. (2000), "Klimaänderung und Anpassungsprozesse im Wintertourismus", Publikation der Ostschweizerischen Geographischen Gesellschaft, Neue Folge – Heft 6, St. Gallen

Burki R. *et al.* (2005), "Climate change and tourism in the Swiss Alps", In: (eds Hall M. and Higham J.) *Aspects of Tourism. Tourism, recreation and climate change*, pp. 155-163.

Casty, C. *et al.* (2005), "Temperature and precipitation variability in the European Alps since 1500", *International Journal of Climatology*, Vol. 25 (14), pp. 1855-1880.

CEC (Commission of the European Communities) (2005), "European Union Solidarity Fund – Annual report 2004", Brussels, December 2005.

CEC (2006), "Proposal for a Directive of the European Parliament and of the Council on the Assessment and management of floods", Brussels, January 2006.

CCR (Caisse Centrale de Réassurance) (2005), "Les Catastrophes naturelles en France – Natural disasters in France", Caisse centrale de Réassurance, Paris, France. Available at http://www.ccr.fr .

Cernusca, A. *et al.* (1990), Auswirkungen von Kunstschnee: eine Kausalanalyse der Belastungsfaktoren. Verhandlungen der Gesellschaft für Ökologie 19: 746-757

CIPRA – Commission Internationale pour la Protection des Alpes (ed.) (2003), "Aufrüstung im Alpinen Wintersport – ein Hintergrundbericht". Available at http://www.alpmedia.net.

CIPRA – Commission Internationale pour la Protection des Alpes (ed.) (2004), "Künstliche Beschneiung im Alpenraum – ein Hintergrundbericht". Available at http://www.alpmedia.net.

Department of Home Affairs (ed.) (1991), "Landschaftseingriffe für den Skisport – Wegleitung zur Berücksichtigung des Natur- und Landschaftschutzes", Berne.

DETEC (Department of Environment, Transport, Energy and Communications) (2006a), *"Cartographie des dangers : les cantons doivent encore fournir de gros efforts"*, Département fédéral de l'Environnement, des Transports, de l'Énergie et de la Communication, Berne, June 2006.

DETEC (2006b), *"Aperçu de l'évolution du permafrost en Suisse"*, Département fédéral de l'Environnement, des Transports, de l'Énergie et de la Communication, Berne, July 2006.

Deutscher Skiverband (2004), "DSV-Atlas Ski Winter 2005", Verlagsgruppe J. Fink GmbH & Co, Ostfildern.

Dietmann T. and Kohler U. (2005), "Die Skipistenuntersuchung Bayern: Landschaftsökologische Untersuchung in den bayrischen Skigebieten. Bayerisches Landesamt für Umweltschutz", Augsburg.

Direction du Tourisme (2002), "Les chiffres clés du tourisme de montagne en France, 3ème edition", Ministère des Transport, de l'Équipement, du Tourisme et de la Mer, France. Service d'Études et d'Aménagement touristique de la montagne.

Direction du Tourisme (2004), "Les chiffres clés du tourisme de montagne en France. 4ème edition", Ministère des Transport, de l'Équipement, du Tourisme et de la Mer, France. Service d'Études et d'Aménagement touristique de la montagne.

Direction du Tourisme (2005), "Le positionnement de l'offre française de sports d'hiver - Note de Synthèse", Ministère des Transport, de l'Équipement, du Tourisme et de la Mer, France. Étude réalisée par le cabinet d'Architecture et Territoire pour le compte de la direction du Tourisme.

Direction du Tourisme (2006), "Les comptes du tourisme. Compte 2005", Ministère des Transport, de l'Équipement, du Tourisme et de la Mer, France. Rapport présenté à la Commission des Comptes du Tourisme, Mai 2006.

Dubois, J.P. and Ceron G. (2003), "Changes in leisure/tourism mobility patterns facing the stake of global warming: the case of France", in A. Montanari and P. Salvà Tomàs (eds.), *Human mobility in a globalizing world*, Special issue of *Belgian Journal of Geography*, pp.103-120.

Dumas *et al.* (2005), "Rapport Particulier sur les Aspects Assuranciels et Institutionnels du Régime CATNAT", Rapport No. 2004-0304-01, Conseil générale des ponts et chaussées, Paris, France, September 2005.

Elsasser, H. and Messerli P. (2001), "The vulnerability of the snow industry in the Swiss Alps", *Journal of Mountain Research and Development*, Vol. 21 (4), pp. 335-339.

Elsasser, H. and Bürki, R. (2002), "Climate change as a threat to tourism in the Alps", *Climate Research*, Vol. 20, pp. 253-257.

EEA (European Environment Agency) (2003), "Mapping the impacts of recent natural disasters and technological accidents in Europe", Environmental Issues, report No 35, Copenhagen, Denmark.

EEA (2005), "Vulnerability and adaptation to climate change in Europe", Technical Report No7/2005, Copenhagen, Denmark.

Fachverband der Seilbahnen Österreich (2005), "Österreichs Seilbahnen voll im Aufwärtstrend. Medienservice Winter 2005/06". Available at http://www.seilbahnen.at.

FAO (Food and Agriculture Organisation) (2001), "Global Forest Fire Assessment 1990-2000", Forestry Department, Forest Resources Assessment Working Paper – 055, Rome, Italy.

Fischer, A., Olefs, M. and Lang, J. (2006), "Adaptation measures to climate change for glacier ski resorts", Poster presented at 9th Österreichischer Klimatag, Vienna, March 16-17th 2006. Abstract available at http://www.austroclim.at.

Fitharris, B. (1995), "The cryosphere: Changes and their impacts", Cambridge University Press, New York, NY, USA, pp.241-265.

Föhn, P. (1990), "Schnee und Lawinen. In: Schnee, Eis und Wasser der Alpen in einer wärmeren Atmosphäre", Internationale Fachtagung, Mitteilungen *VAW ETH Zurich* No. 108, pp. 33-48.

Frei, Ch. (2004), "Die Klimazukunft der Schweiz – eine probabilistische Projektion". Available at http://www.occc.ch/Products/CH2050/ch2050_scenario_d.html (accessed: June 20th, 2006).

Frei, C. and C. Schär 1998, "A precipitation climatology of the Alps from high-resolution rain-gauge observations", *International Journal of Climatology*, Vol. 18 (8), pp. 873 – 900.

Frei C. and C. Schär (2001), "Detection probability of trends in rare events: Theory and application to heavy precipitation in the Alpine region", *Journal of Climate*, Vol. 14, pp.1568-1584.

Glass B. *et al.* (2000), "Retour d'expérience sur l'avalanche du 9 février 1999 à Montroc, commune de Chamonix", Inspection Générale de l'environnement, Ministère de l'Aménagement du Territoire et de l'Environnement, Affaire n° IGE 00 002.

Gruber, S., M. Hoelzle, and W. Haeberli (2004), "Permafrost thaw and destabilization of Alpine rock walls in the hot summer of 2003", *Geophysical Research Letters*, Vol.31, L13504.

Guillot, J. (2006), "Herausforderungen für den Tourismus", In: Lebensministerium (ed): Klimawandel im Alpenraum – Auswirkungen und Herausforderungen, Vienna, pp.39-41.

Haeberli, W. (1992), "Construction, environmental problems and natural hazards in periglacial mountain belts", *Permafrost and Periglacial Processes*, Vol. 3, pp. 111-124.

Haeberli, W. and M. Hoelzle (1995), "Application of inventory data for estimating characteristics of and regional climate-change effects on mountain glaciers: a pilot study with the European Alps", *Annals of Glaciology*, Vol. 21, pp.206-212.

Hoelzle, M. and W. Haeberli (1995), "Simulating the effects of mean annual air-temperature changes on permafrost distribution and glacier size: an example from the Upper Engadin, Swiss Alps", *Annals of Glaciology*, Vol. 21, pp.399-405.

Haeberli, W. and Beniston, M. (1998), "Climate change and its impacts on glaciers and permafrost in the Alps", *Ambio*, Vol. 27, pp. 258-265.

Hall, M.C. and Higham, J. (eds) (2005), "Tourism, recreation and climate change", Aspects of Tourism 22, Channel View Publications, Clevedon/Buffalo/Toronto.

Hantel, M., Ehrendorfer, M. and Haslinger, A. (2000), "Climate sensitivity of snow cover duration in Austria", *International Journal of Climatology*, Vol. 20, pp. 615-640.

Harris, C. *et al.* (2003), "Warming Permafrost in European Mountains", *Global and Planetary Change*, Vol. 39, pp.215–225.

Hasslacher, P. 2005. Gletscherschutz – ein wichtiger Baustein der Alpinen Raumordnung. In: Oesterreichischer Alpenverein (ed): Bedrohte Alpengletscher, Alpine Raumordnung Nr. 27, Innsbruck, 7-15.

Heimann D. and V. Sept (2000), "Climate Change Estimates of Summer Temperature and Precipitation in the Alpine Region", *Theoretical and Applied Climatology*, Vol. 66 (1-2), pp 1-12.

Hyll, W., N.Vetters, and F. Prettenthaler (2003), "What is the Optimal Mix of Insurance, Public Risk Pooling and Alternative Risk Transfer Mechanisms", Project StartClim.8, University of Graz, Graz, Austria.

IPCC (Intergovernmental Panel on Climate Change) (2001), "The IPCC Third Assessment Report, Volumes I (Science), II (Impacts and Adaptation) and III (Mitigation Strategies)". Cambridge, New York, Cambridge University Press.

Jomelli, V. *et al.* (2004), "Geomorphic Variations of Debris Flows and Recent Climatic Change in the French Alps", *Climatic Change*, Vol. 64, pp. 77-102.

Kamber, M. (2006), "Climate change and property insurance: perspective from the Swiss public insurers", OECD – Wengen 2006 workshop: Adaptation to the impacts of climate change in the European Alps, Wengen, Switzerland, October 4-6.

Kammer, P.M. (2002), "Floristic changes in subAlpine grasslands after 22 years of artificial snowing", *Journal for Nature Conservation*, Vol.10, pp. 109-123.

Klawa , M., and U. Ulbrich (2003), "A model for the estimation of storm losses and the identification of severe winter storms in Germany", *Natural Hazards and Earth System Sciences*, Vol.3, pp. 725–732.

König, U. and Abegg, B. (1997), "Impacts of climate change on winter tourism in the Swiss Alps", *Journal of Sustainable Tourism*, Vol. 5(1), pp. 46-58.

König, U. (1998), "Tourism in a warmer world", Implications of climate change due to enhanced Greenhouse effect for the ski industry in the Australian Alps, Zurich.

Laternser, M. and Schneebeli, M. (2003), "Long-term snow climate trends of the Swiss Alps 1931-1999", *International Journal of Climatology*, Vol. 23, pp.733-750.

Leutwyler, C. (2006), "Bettenburg mitten auf der Alp", In: Tages-Anzeiger, July, 24th 2006.

Liu, X. and B. Chen (2000), "Climatic Warming in the Tibetan Plateau During Recent Decades", *International Journal of Climatology*, Vol. 20 (14), pp. 1729-42.

Loster, T. (2005), "Strategic management of climate change – Options for the insurance industry", In *Weather catastrophes and climate change - Is there still hope for us?*, Geo Risks Research, MunichRe, Munich, Germany, pp.236-243.

Martin, E., Brun, E. and Durand, Y. (1994), "Sensitivity of the French Alps snow cover to the variation of climatic variables", *Annales Geophysicae*, Vol. 12, pp. 469-477.

Mathis, P., Siegrist, D. and Kessler, R. (2003), "Neue Skigebiete in der Schweiz? Planungsstand und Finanzierung von touristischen Neuerschliessungen unter besonderer Berücksichtigung der Kantone", Berne.

Matulla, C. *et al.* (2005), "Outstanding past decadal-scale climate events in the Greater Alpine Region analysed by 250 years data and model run", GKSS-Forschungszentrum, Geesthacht.

Middlekoop, H. *et al.* (2001), "Impact of climate change on hydrological regimes and water resources management in the Rhine basin", Climatic *Change*, Vol. 49 (1-2), pp. 105-128.

Mountain Wilderness (2005), "Enneigement artificiel: Eau Secours!" Available at: http://france.mountainwilderness.org/download/document/TAPCanons.pdf

Mühll, D.V. *et al.* (2004), "Permafrost in Switzerland 2000/2001 and 2001/2002", Glaciological Report (Permafrost) No. 2/3, Glaciological Commission (GC) of the Swiss Academy of Sciences (SAS), Institute of Geography, University of Zurich, Zurich, Switzerland.

Neuhäuser, V. (2006), "Tourismusbranche ohne Fantasie?", In: CIPRA Info 80: 7.

OcCC (Organe consultatif sur les changements climatiques) (2003), "Extreme Events and Climate Change", Bern, Switzerland.

Odermatt, M. (2005), "Frischer Schnee aus Staatskanonen", In: Tages-Anzeiger, February, 7th 2005: 19.

OECD (Organisation pour la Coopération et le Développement Économique) (2006), "France- Politique de Prévention et d'Indemnisation des Dommages Liés aux Inondations", Études de l'OCDE sur la gestion des risques, Paris, France.

ÖROK (Austrian Conference on Spatial Planning) (2005), "Präventiver Umgang mit Naturgefahren in der Raumordnung, Materialienband", Vienna.

Pechlaner & Tschurtschenthaler (2003), "Tourism policy, tourism organizations and change management in Alpine regions and destinations: a European perspective", *Current issues in tourism* , Vol. 6(6), pp. 508-538.

Pfund, C. (1993) "Die Seilbahnen in Zahlen", Presentation at the 23rd Annual Meeting of the Association of Swiss Cableways (Seilbahnen Schweiz), Champéry (Switzerland), Sept. 16th, 1993.

PLANAT (National Platform for Natural Hazards) (2004), "*Stratégie Dangers naturels en Suisse - Rapport de Synthèse*", Office fédéral des eaux et de la géologie, Bienne.

Prettenthaler F., and N. Vetters (2006), "Adapting National Risk Transfer systems: How much regulation for the insurance markets?", OECD – Wengen 2006 workshop: Adaptation to the impacts of climate change in the European Alps, Wengen, Switzerland, October 4-6.

Pröbstl, U. (2006), "Kunstschnee und Umwelt. Entwicklung und Auswirkungen der technischen Beschneiung", Berne.

PRUDENCE (Predition of regional scenarios and uncertainties for defining European climate change risks and effects [European Climate Project]). Information available at http://prudence.dmi.dk.

Prudent, G. (2006), "Climatic change in the Alpine arc: focus on natural hazards", Consultant report for the OECD, Paris, France.

Reinhard, M., M. Rebetez, and R. Schlaepfer (2005), "Recent climate change: Rethinking drought in the context of Forest Fire Research in Ticino, South of Switzerland", *Theoretical and Applied Climatology*, Vol. 82, pp. 17-25.

Richard, D., and M. Gay (2003), GLACIORISK Final report - Survey and Prevention of Extreme Glaciological Hazards. Available at http://glaciorisk.grenoble.cemagref.fr.

Rixen, C., Stoeckli, V. and Ammann, W. (2003), "Does artificial snow production affect soil and vegetation of ski pistes? A review", *Perspectives in Plant Ecology, Evolution and Systematics*, Vol.5 (4), pp. 210-230.

Scherrer, S. C., Appenzeller, C. and Laternser M. (2004), "Trends in Swiss Alpine snow days: The role of local- and large-scale climate variability", *Geophysical Research Letters*, Vol. 31, L13215.

Schmid, A. (2006), "Gut gekühlte Gletscher halten etwas länger", in: NZZ am Sonntag, July 16th 2006, pp.21.

Scott, D., McBoyle, G. and Mills, B. (2003), "Climate change and the skiing industry in southern Ontario (Canada): exploring the importance of snowmaking as a technical adaptation", *Climate Research* Vol. 23, pp. 171-181.

Scott, D. (2006), "Global Environmental Change and Mountain Tourism", in: Gössling, St. and Hall, C. M. (eds.): Tourism and Global Environmental Change, London, pp.54-75.

Scott, D., McBoyle, G., Mills, B. and Minogue, A. (2006), "Climate change and the sustainability of ski-based tourism in eastern North America: a reassessment", *Journal of Sustainable Tourism*, Vol. 14(4), pp. 376-398.

Scott D., McBoyle G. and Minogue A. (In press), "Climate change and Quebec's ski industry", *Global Environmental Change*.

SEATM (Service d'Etudes et d'Aménagement Touristique de la Montagne) (2003), "Bilan des investissements dans les domaines skiables français en 2003", *Aménagement & Montagne* No. 179, October/November 2003.

Seifert, W. (2004), Klimaänderungen und (Winter-)Tourismus im Fichtelgebirge – Auswirkungen, Wahrnehmungen und Ansatzpunkte zukünftiger touristischer Entwicklung. Arbeitsmaterialien zur Raumordnung und Raumplanung, Heft 233, Bayreuth.

Seilbahnen Schweiz (ed). (2003), "Schweizer Seilbahnen – wohin? Bericht zur Lage der Seilbahnbranche in der Schweiz, Berne.

Seilbahnen Schweiz (ed). (2005a), "Seilbahnen der Schweiz – Fakten und Zahlen 2004, Berne.

Seilbahnen Schweiz (ed). (2005b), "Seilbahnverbände fördern den Wintersportnachwuchs. Press release, available at http://wwwseilbahnen.org

Seiler, W. (2006), "Der Klimawandel im Alpenraum: Trends, Auswirkungen und Herausforderungen". In: Lebensministerium (ed): Klimawandel im Alpenraum – Auswirkungen und Herausforderungen, Vienna, pp. 7-20.

Shreshtha *et al.* (1999), "Maximum Temperature Trends in the Himalaya and Its Vicinity: An Analysis Based on Temperature Records from Nepal fro the Period 1971-94", *Journal of Climate*, Vol. 12 (9), pp.2775-89.

Simon, C. (2006), "Eine neue Politik für die Tourismusorte der Isère/F", In: CIPRA Info 80 pp. 9.

Stoffel, M., and M. Beniston (2006), "On the incidence of debris flows from the early Little Ice Age to a future greenhouse climate: A case study from the Swiss Alps", *Geophysical Research Letters*, Vol. 33, L16404.

SwissInfo (2001), "Village pioneers defences against global warming", Swiss Broadcasting Corporation, September 7, 2001. Available at www.swissinfo.org.

SwissInfo (2003), "Pontresina becomes village of the dammed", Swiss Broadcasting Corporation, August 13, 2003. Available at www.swissinfo.org.

SwissRe, (2006), "The effects of climate change: Storm damage in Europe on the rise", Focus Report, SwissRe, Zurich, Switzerland.

Switzerland (2005), "Fourth National Communication to the UNFCCC", Swiss Agency for the Environment, Forest and Landscape; Berne, Switzerland.

von Ungern-Sternberg, Thomas (2004), "Efficient Monopolies: The Limits of Competition in the European Property Insurance Market", Oxford University Press, Oxford, UK.

Umweltbundesamt with Max Planck Institute for Meteorology (eds) (2006), "Künftige Klimaänderungen in Deutschland – Regionale Projektionen für das 21", Jahrhundert. Hintergrundpapier April 2006. Available at http://www.umweltbundesamt.de/klimaschutz (accessed: June 9th, 2006).

Urbanska, K. M. (1997), "Restoration ecology research above the timberline: colonization of safety islands on a machine-graded Alpine ski run", *Biodiversity and Conservation*, Vol. 4, pp. 1655-1670.

Viner D. and Agnew M. (1999), "Climate Change and its impacts on tourism", Report prepared for WWF-UK.

Wielke, L.-M., Haimberger, L. and Hantel, M. (2004), "Snow cover duration in Switzerland compared to Austria", *Meteorologische Zeitschrift*, Vol. 13, pp. 13-17.

Wipf, S., Rixen, C., Fischer, M., Schmid, B. and Stoeckli, V. (2005), Effects of ski piste preparation on Alpine vegetation. Journal of Applied Ecology 42: 306-316

Wirtschaftsministerium Baden-Württemberg (ed). (2005), "Nachhaltige Entwicklung des Schneesports und des Wintersporttourismus in Baden-Württemberg", Ein Leitfaden für Politik, Sport, Kommunen and touristische Leistungsträger, Offenburg.

Witmer, U. (1986), "Erfassung, Bearbeitung und Kartierung von Schneedaten in der Schweiz", Geographica Bernensia G25.

Wolfsegger, C., Gössling, S. and Scott, D. (In press), "Climate change risk appraisal in the Austrian ski industry", Submitted to Tourism Review International.

WWF (World Wildlife Fund) Italia (2006a), "Alpi e turismo: trovare il punto di equilibrio", Available at: http://www.wwf.it/ambiente/dossier/Alpi_e_Turismo.pdf

WWF Italia (2006b), "Alpi, turismo e ambiente: alla ricerca di un equilibrio", WWF Report, pp.137.

Zebisch, M. *et al.* (2005), "Climate change in Germany: vulnerability and adaptation of climate sensitive sectors", Research report on behalf of the Federal Environmental Agency (Umweltbundesamt). Available at http://www.umweltbundesamt.de.

Zemp, M. *et al.* (2006), "Alpine glaciers to disappear within decades?" *Geophysical Research Letters,* Vol. 33, L13504.

Zemp, M. *et al.* (In press), "Glacier fluctuations in the European Alps 1850-2000: an overview and spatio-temporal analysis of available data", in: Orlove, B., Wieganddt, E. and B. Luckman (eds.): *The darkening peaks: Glacial retreat in scientific and social context,* University of California Press.

Zeng, L. (2000), "Weather derivates and weather insurance: concept, application, and analysis", *Bulletin of the American Meteorological Society*, Vol. 81, pp. 2075-2082.

Websites

AlpMedia. Le service d'informations pour les Alpes. Available at: www.alpmedia.net.

ANPNC. Le site Internet de l'Association Nationale des Professionnels de la Neige de Culture. Available at: www.anpnc.com.

Austrian Federal Ministry of Agriculture, Forestry, Environment and Water Management, Water management: www.hochwasserrisiko.at.

DPPR, Direction de la Prévention des Pollutions et des Risques, Paris France : www.ecologie.gouv.fr.

Glaciorisk project: http://glaciorisk. grenoble.cemagref.fr.

IRV/UIR, Intercantonal Reinsurance Union, Bern, Switzerland: www.kgvonline.ch/.

Ministère des Transport, de l'Équipement, du Tourisme et de la Mer: www.tourisme.gouv.fr.

Osterreichischer AlpenVerein: www.alpenverein.at.

Projekt Hochwasserschutz Samedan 2002 bis 2006: www.flaz.ch.

Promethhee database: www.promethee.com.

ProNatura. Conservation Organisation. Available at: www.pronatura.ch.

Verband Deutscher Seilbahnen: www.seilbahnen.de.

APPENDIX 1

Results: snow-reliable ski areas

A.1 Table 1. **Present and future natural snow-reliability of ski areas in the European Alps**

Number and percentages of ski areas that will remain snow-reliable compared with number of present-day ski areas

A = Austria, CH = Switzerland, D = Germany, F = France, I = Italy

	Region	Ski areas	Present	+1 °C	+2 °C	+4 °C
A	Vorarlberg	25	19 *(76%)*	16 *(64%)*	12 *(48%)*	3 *(12%)*
	Tirol/Tyrol	79	75 *(95%)*	61 *(77%)*	45 *(57%)*	23 *(29%)*
	Salzburg	39	35 *(90%)*	29 *(74%)*	24 *(62%)*	9 *(23%)*
	Kärnten/Carinthia	24	20 *(83%)*	15 *(63%)*	14 *(58%)*	7 *(29%)*
	Oberösterreich	11	7 *(64%)*	4 *(36%)*	2 *(18%)*	0
	Niederösterreich	13	9 *(69%)*	2 *(15%)*	1 *(8%)*	0
	Steiermark/Styria	37	34 *(92%)*	26 *(70%)*	17 *(46%)*	5 *(14%)*
CH	Eastern CH	12	10 *(83%)*	7 *(58%)*	7 *(58%)*	1 *(8%)*
	Alpes VD+FR	17	17 *(100%)*	11 *(65%)*	9 *(53%)*	1 *(6%)*
	Bernese Oberland	26	25 *(96%)*	22 *(85%)*	16 *(62%)*	3 *(12%)*
	Central CH	20	18 *(90%)*	15 *(75%)*	11 *(55%)*	4 *(20%)*
	Ticino	4	4 *(100%)*	3 *(75%)*	2 *(50%)*	0
	Grisons	36	36 *(100%)*	35 *(97%)*	35 *(97%)*	30 *(83%)*
	Valais/Wallis	49	49 *(100%)*	49 *(100%)*	49 *(100%)*	39 *(80%)*
D	Oberbayern	20	18 *(90%)*	8 *(40%)*	3 *(15%)*	1 *(5%)*
	Schwaben/Allgäu	19	9 *(47%)*	3 *(16%)*	2 *(11%)*	0
F	Alpes Maritimes	9	9 *(100%)*	7 *(78%)*	2 *(22%)*	1 *(11%)*
	Drôme	4	1 *(25%)*	0	0	0
	Haute-Provence	10	10 *(100%)*	9 *(90%)*	7 *(70%)*	1 *(10%)*
	Isère	19	19 *(100%)*	16 *(84%)*	12 *(63%)*	7 *(37%)*
	Hautes Alpes	27	27 *(100%)*	24 *(89%)*	19 *(70%)*	9 *(33%)*
	Savoie	42	42 *(100%)*	40 *(95%)*	38 *(90%)*	30 *(71%)*
	Haute Savoie	37	35 *(95%)*	27 *(73%)*	18 *(49%)*	7 *(19%)*
I	Piemonte	18	18 *(100%)*	16 *(89%)*	15 *(83%)*	5 *(28%)*
	Lombardia	6	6 *(100%)*	6 *(100%)*	5 *(83%)*	4 *(67%)*
	Trentino	20	19 *(95%)*	16 *(80%)*	14 *(70%)*	3 *(15%)*
	South Tyrol	32	31 *(97%)*	27 *(84%)*	20 *(63%)*	7 *(22%)*
	Friuli/Venezia/Giulia	11	7 *(64%)*	6 *(55%)*	5 *(45%)*	2 *(18%)*

A.1. Figure 1. **Percentage of naturally snow-reliable ski areas in the European Alps under present and future climate conditions**

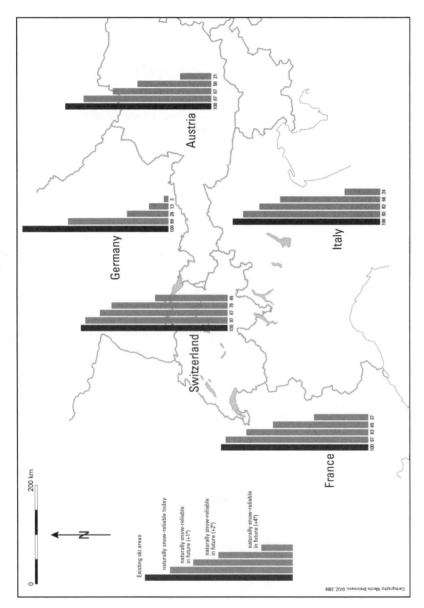

A.1. Figure 2. **Number of naturally snow-reliable ski areas in the Swiss Alps under present and future climate conditions**

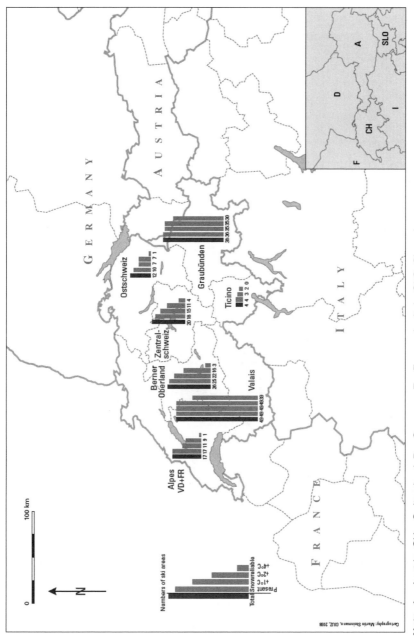

Cartography: Martin Steinmann, GRIZ, 2006

Note: A = Austria, CH = Switzerland, D = Germany, F = France, I = Italy, SLO=Slovenia.

A.1. Figure 3. **Number of naturally snow-reliable ski areas in the French Alps under present and future climate conditions**

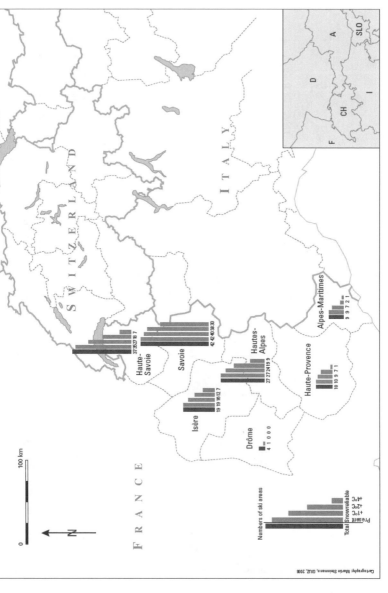

Note: A = Austria, CH = Switzerland, D = Germany, F = France, I = Italy, SLO=Slovenia.

A.1. Figure 4. **Number of naturally snow-reliable ski areas in the Italian Alps under present and future climate conditions**

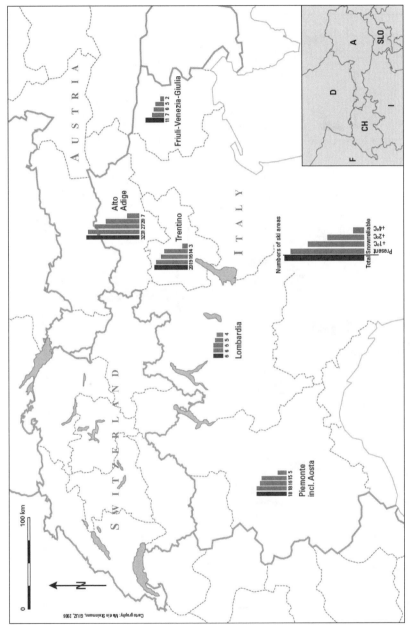

Cartography: Martin Beniston, GIUZ, 2006

Note: A = Austria, CH = Switzerland, D = Germany, F = France, I = Italy, SLO=Slovenia.

A.1. Figure 5. Number of naturally snow-reliable ski areas in Austria and Germany (Bavaria) under present and future climate conditions

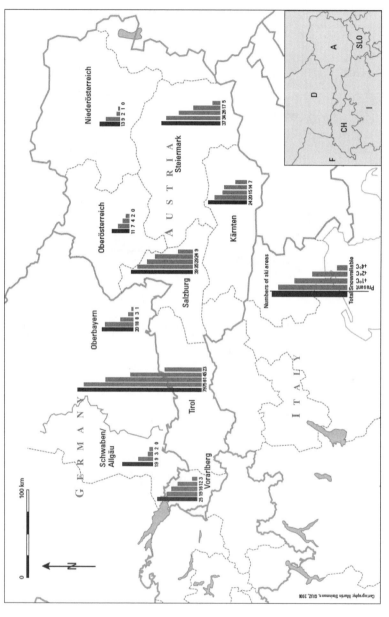

Note: A = Austria, CH = Switzerland, D = Germany, F = France, I = Italy, SLO=Slovenia.

APPENDIX 2

Tourism stakeholders' perception of climate change

Several surveys examining the perception of climate change by tourism representatives have been conducted in Switzerland over the last decade (see Abegg, 1996; Behringer *et al.*, 2000; Bürki, 2000). These surveys found that tourism stakeholders recognize that climate change is a problem for winter tourism and are familiar with the potential consequences of climate change for winter tourism. However, tourism stakeholders appear to view potential climate change as being of minor importance. They also believe that climate change is presented in a highly exaggerated form by the media, as well as in science and politics. The discussions held in the focus groups carried out during these surveys clearly revealed an ambivalent relationship to climate change. On the one hand, the representatives strongly distrust the information disseminated about climate change and play down its potential consequences. On the other hand, they use climate change to legitimate forward strategies. Climate change and global warming, together with international competition, have been used as the key arguments for constructing artificial snow-making facilities, as well as for extending existing ski runs and opening new ones in high-Alpine sites (at an altitude above 2 500 m).

The latest results stem from a survey in Austria by Wolfsegger *et al.* (in press). Wolfsegger *et al.* found that the managers of low-elevation ski areas (i.e. at least 50% of the skiable terrain below 1 500 m a.s.l.) are aware of the challenges. A clear majority expects at least some substantial changes to occur, as only 25% of respondents believe that the climate will remain stable. The most probable climatic changes anticipated by the ski area managers are increased extreme weather events and less snow. 39% of respondents felt it was very to moderately probable that the ski season would be shortened, but this does not necessarily mean that fewer tourists are believed to visit the area. Furthermore, a majority of the ski managers did not perceive climate change to be a substantial threat, because most believed that adaptation strategies, such as snow-making, would be sufficient to cope with climate change in the 21st century. Without further adaptation, 47% of the ski area managers believed that their businesses would not be economically viable in 15 years. With further adaptation though, a vast majority of the managers (82%) thought that their ski operations would remain economically viable for at least another 30-45 years. In general, it appears that most ski area operators strongly believe in their ability to adapt to potential impacts of climate change.

Wolfsegger *et al.* (in press) also asked the Austrian ski area operators to rate the appropriateness of a range of possible climate change adaptation strategies. With regard to technological adaptation, snow-making was considered the most appropriate strategy to cope with climate change, deemed "very appropriate" by 90% of respondents. Moving or expanding ski runs to higher elevation was the second most preferred option, followed by avoiding southern exposure of ski slopes. The area managers were divided in their opinions of whether snow-making with chemical additives and improving seasonal weather forecasts were appropriate or inappropriate adaptations. With regard to business strategies, "sharing the cost of snow-making with the accommodation sector" was considered the most appropriate option, followed by "joining ski conglomerates", "diversification of winter products", "diversification of product throughout the season", and "enhanced marketing". In addition, "governmental subsidies for snow-making" and "reviewing environmental regulations" were preferred policy options, while climate change mitigation through lobbying to reduce emissions of greenhouse gases and "governmental support in case of economic losses" were seen as moderately appropriate.

APPENDIX 3

The future skiers market: results from analogue studies and surveys

The existing literature on the potential reaction of skiers can be divided into analogue studies and surveys. Past warm winters can be used as analogues, as they might represent what a normal winter is expected to be like under a changed climate. Abegg, (1996) investigated the impacts of three snow-deficient winters at the end of the 1980s in Switzerland (winters 1987/88 to 1989/90). These winters were generally too warm, and up to the end of January or mid-February extremely snow-deficient. Switzerland had seen snow-deficient winters before, but to experience three consecutive winters with such poor snow conditions was most unusual. The lack of snow left a clear mark on the ski industry. The earnings of ski area operators decreased by an average of 20% compared to the "normal" winter of 1986/87. Ski and snowboard instructors, as well as the winter sports retail industry, were also seriously affected. However, the impacts differed greatly among regions. Smaller ski areas at lower and medium elevations suffered most (there were even a few bankruptcies) while a number of large ski areas above 1 700 m achieved good and even first-rate results due to the lack of snow at lower and medium elevations, indicating the skiers' movement to higher and more snow-reliable sites (see also König and Abegg, 1997). The slump in the hotel and holiday-apartment trade was less pronounced, as they also accommodate non-skiers. Hotel rooms and holiday apartments also tend to be booked in advance. However, the question does arise, as to how long tourists will remain loyal and keep returning to a certain location if they are repeatedly confronted with inadequate snow conditions.

A survey in eastern North America was also carried out examining skier demand for the two winters of 2000/01 and 2001/02 (record-high temperatures during this winter) and using this as an analogue for the 2050s (under mid-range scenario) (see Scott, 2006). The results for the 2050s indicate a lower than expected decline in skiing demand. This might be explained by the behavioural adaptation of the skiers: a higher utilization of the ski area (more frequent visits during a shorter season). However in this study the impacts of climate change were buffered by the heavy use of snow-making equipment.

In contrast to the stakeholders' point of view (see Annex 2), skiers appear to perceive climate change as a serious problem for the tourism industry. A survey conducted at five ski resorts in Central Switzerland by Bürki (2000) reveals that 83% of the respondents believe that climate change will threaten the ski industry, and almost half of them believe that this will happen between 2000 and 2030. In response to the question "Where and how often would you ski if you knew that the next five winters would have very little natural snow?" the majority of skiers (58%) replied that they would ski with the same frequency (30% at the same resort and 28% at a more snow-reliable resort), while almost one-third (32%) of respondents indicated they would ski less often and 4% would stop skiing altogether. With more than one-third of the sampled ski market skiing less or quitting, the implications of climate change for the future demand of skiing in Switzerland would be significant. A similar survey was conducted in the Snowy Mountains of Australia and obtained similar results (see König, 1998).

Skiers were also asked, what they thought about different adaptation strategies. Roughly half of the skiers surveyed deemed snow-making and/or the extension of ski areas to higher elevations as important. Less important were attractions and events in the ski resort and activities that are not dependent on snow cover (Bürki, 2000). These results stand in sharp contrast to the findings from Australia (König, 1998), where nearly all skiers (up to 92%) consider snow-making as an important tool to secure ski operation. The same is true for North America (Scott, 2006), where snow-making has been an integral part of the ski area operations for many years – just as in Australia. In Switzerland, though, many skiers seem to remain skeptical regarding the use of snow-making equipment.

APPENDIX 4

Adaptation trends, limits and synergies

Adaptation Strategies	Examples of observed trends	Limits to strategies	Potential Conflicts/Synergies
Technological: • Landscaping and slope development	• 27% of skiable domain in Bavaria (999 out of 3 665ha) modified through landscaping and slope development. 75% of these changes involved machine grading and 15% was due to forest clearing.	• Damaging management activity with greater consequences at higher altitudes. • Unsustainable strategy in terms of integrated tourism policy as negative effect on attractiveness of Alpine environment may negatively impact summer tourism.	• Environmental impacts: increased risk of erosion; impact on biodiversity and vegetation cover (e.g., re-vegetation of graded sites difficult to achieve).
• Going higher and facing north	• In 2001 there were 155 extension projects in the Alps as well as 48 projects to connect existing ski areas and 26 projects to build new ski areas in formerly untouched areas. • "Savognin 1900" project being considered in Switzerland: development of a new resort in a high valley and extension of ski area of Savognin by one third including Piz Mez at an altitude of 2 718 m.	• North-facing slopes unattractive to skiers. • Limited and un-extendable altitudinal ranges of many ski areas. • Possible increase risk of avalanches and heavy winds at higher altitudes. • Extension of ski areas is very costly: a survey found that high mountain extensions in Switzerland cost between CHF 40 and 49 million.	• Opposition from environmental groups, as high elevation mountain environments are particularly sensitive to disturbance. • Construction of new ski lifts and development of new ski areas will increase pollution (increased traffic linked to tourism) and contribute to GHG emissions (the French Institute for the Environment (Ifen) estimated that the energy consumption of 4000 lifts during a winter season was between 571 and 734GWh, equivalent to a ¼ or 1/3 of the annual energy production of a nuclear plant).

APPENDIX 4 : Adaptation trends, limits and synergies (continued)

Adaptation Strategies	Examples of observed trends	Limits to strategies	Potential Conflicts/Synergies
• Glacier skiing	• In 2003 a new ski lift was inaugurated on the south-facing Hockengrat glacier in Switzerland. • Possible future developments of ski areas in Austria on the glaciers of Pitzal and Kaunertal.	• Unsustainable strategy in the long-term because of climate change: by 2050 it is estimated that 75% of glaciers in Swiss Alps will have disappeared and by 2100 the whole Alps could lose almost all of their glacier cover. • Changing preferences among summer tourists leading to a decline in summer glacier skiing.	• Environmental impacts of opening new ski areas on glaciers; opposition from environmental groups.
• Use of white sheets to protect glaciers from melting	• In Tyrol (Austria) 28 ha covered by white sheets (about 3% of glacier ski area). • 6 ha of the Pitzal glacier in Austria are covered by sheets. • A variety of places in Switzerland use white sheets on their glaciers: Saas Fee and Verbier (Canton of Valais/Wallis), Engelberg and Andermatt (Central Switzerland), and Laax (Canton of Grisons).	• White sheets will not save the glaciers: very much a short-term strategy. • High costs mean that only the most vulnerable part of glaciers can be protected.	• Opposition from environmental groups such as Greenpeace and Pro Natura.

APPENDIX 4 : Adaptation trends, limits and synergies (continued)

Adaptation Strategies	Examples of observed trends	Limits to strategies	Potential Conflicts/Synergies
• Snow-making	• Percentage of total skiable terrain covered by snow-making in each country: 50% for Austria (11 500ha), 18% for Switzerland (3 960ha), 11.5% for the German Alps, 15.5% for the French Alps (3 222ha), and 40% for Italy (9 000ha). • Austria and the Italian Alps have the greatest share of ski runs equipped with artificial snow-making equipment in the European Alps. • 135 ski stations in the French Alps equipped with artificial snow-making facilities • In the French Alps snow cannons have in the last couple of years been installed on the glaciers of Tignes and Val d'Isère and the resort of Alpe d'Huez is planning on using artificial snow on its glacier.	• Costs of snow-making will increase under global warming, as more energy and water will be needed to produce snow under warmer temperatures. • Snow cannons ineffective at temperatures above -2 °C, while the use of additives (e.g., Snomax) and the "all-weather" snow cannon involve significantly higher costs. • Many of the small and medium size resorts will not be able to afford the increased costs involved in snow-making under warmer temperatures and may lose in market share as skiers move to more snow-reliable ski resorts.	• The large quantities of water required for snow-making are putting an enormous strain on water resources as the water used for snow-making is withdrawn at a time when water is scarce in the mountains and competes with other water uses such as the need for drinking water and the generation of hydroelectric power. • Water withdrawal for snow-making from drinking water reserves, watercourses or mountain reservoirs has negative impacts: it can lead to cuts in the water supply system, reduce water levels of watercourses at critical times of the year and therefore affect aquatic life, can be very destructive on the environment and the Alpine landscape. • Mountain reservoirs are also vulnerable to flooding, rockfalls and avalanches, risks which might increase under climate change. • The use of artificial snow and additives can have negative impacts on Alpine vegetation. • The considerable amount of noise generated by the snow cannons appear to have an effect on the habitat choice and activities of wild animals. • High energy use of snow cannons contributes to GHG emissions and is therefore contributing to the climate change problem.

APPENDIX 4 : Adaptation trends, limits and synergies (continued)

Adaptation Strategies	Examples of observed trends	Limits to strategies	Potential Conflicts/Synergies
Behavioural: • Operational practices	• Some small and medium-size ski resorts at low altitudes have already had to alter the timing of the opening of the season. • In Bavaria, there were plans to create a small "summer ski area" over 2 ha at an altitude of 1 000 m using non-snow surfaces.	• Increasing utilisation levels will only be effective if skier satisfaction can be maintained.	• A reduced ski season may have a negative impact on the economy: for example the restaurant and accommodation sectors may lose out by having fewer tourists in the early and late seasons as some hotels may not be able to increase their capacity to accommodate more tourists during the peak season.
• Financial and Marketing Tools (snow insurance, weather derivatives and marketing incentives)	• Ski resorts are promoting the altitudinal range of their ski areas: Isola 2000, Zillertal 3000.	• Insurance premiums may become too expensive for ski resorts: examples of the use of snow insurance in the United States show that insurance premiums have increased substantially in the last few years – a possible indication of the adaptation of this insurance product by the financial sector – and this has resulted in large ski corporations no longer applying for weather insurance.	
• Financial Support	The local authority of St. Moritz, Canton of Grisons, spent CHF 2.3 million last year to run the transport facilities they own in the ski areas. • In Melchsee-Frutt, Central Switzerland, the local authorities paid for a new chairlift incurring a total cost of CHF 8.5 million.	• Under climate change the need for financial support is likely to increase and ski area operators believe that costs, especially of snow-making, should be shared between all those who benefit (including accommodation industry and whole community). This may lead to strong opposition by the communities.	• This financial support does not always take into consideration the issues of sustainable development and nature conservation or the implications of climate change.

APPENDIX 4 : Adaptation trends, limits and synergies (continued)

Adaptation Strategies	Examples of observed trends	Limits to strategies	Potential Conflicts/Synergies
• Financial Support (*cont.*)	• In Gstaad, Bernese Oberland, about CHF 70 million are necessary to finance the renewal of existing transport facilities, of which 67 million were paid for by the municipality of Saanen and the Cantons of Berne and Vaud.		
	• An analysis of extension projects in Switzerland (1993 to 2001) showed that it was the Cantons that covered the largest part of the investment costs (42%), followed by the banks and the ski area operators themselves (21% each).		
• Cooperation and mergers	• Regional cooperations offering a single ski pass for several ski areas are occurring throughout the Alps.		
	• Merger of "Lenzerheide Bergbahnen Danis Stätz AG" and "Rothornbahn & Scalottas AG" to form a new company called "Lenzerheide Bergbahnen". This company is now the third largest cableway company in the Canton of Grisons, Switzerland, with total revenues of CHF 35 million.		

APPENDIX 4 : Adaptation trends, limits and synergies (continued)

Adaptation Strategies	Examples of observed trends	Limits to strategies	Potential Conflicts/Synergies
• Winter revenue diversification	• Investment in diversification activities: 2 500 km of groomed winter hiking trails in Switzerland; 500 toboggan runs in Austria; and countless opportunities for snowshoeing all over the Alps. • 48% of visitors to winter sports resorts in Italy don't ski or snowboard.	• Tourists may take advantage of non-snow offers but often they do not visit the resort because of these complementary offers. • Non-snow related offers cannot carry the winter industry, as there is no activity available that could substitute the revenue generating power of traditional winter sports. • Ski operators will benefit less from diversification then hoteliers and restaurant owners who cater for all tourists.	• Conflict with mountain agriculture as new developments may take away land previously used for agriculture.
• All year tourism	• *Contrats de Développement Diversifié* being introduced in the Isère. • *Contrats de Plan Etat Région* (CPERs) with a focus on medium-altitude resorts were launched in the Rhône-Alpes Region. • CPER and European Union financed 'Mountain Contracts' which aim to develop regional tourism potential by promoting all year tourism.	• Cableway operators won't benefit as much from seasonal diversification as hoteliers and restaurant owners. • Climate change will have negative impacts on summer tourism: for example the retreat of glaciers will severely affect the attractiveness of the mountain environment. • Some summer tourist attractions will also disappear such as ice caves and summer ski areas.	• Conflict with mountain agriculture: tourism activities may take away land previously used for agriculture. • Increase the dependence of the local population on tourism (may be unsustainable in the long-term) by reducing/removing a potential income-earning opportunity.

APPENDIX 4 : Adaptation trends, limits and synergies (continued)

Adaptation Strategies	Examples of observed trends	Limits to strategies	Potential Conflicts/Synergies
• Withdrawal from ski tourism	• The ski area at Gschwender Horn in Immenstadt, Bavaria, had its ski facilities dismantled and ski runs re-naturalised in the 1990s and is now used for summer and winter tourism (hiking, mountain biking, snowshoeing and ski touring). • Free coach service, established by the "Gemeindenetzwerk Okomodell Achental e.V.", to transport skiers from 8 different communities in Bavaria and Tyrol to the most snow-reliable ski resort within the network area.		• In many ski resorts winter tourism represents the major source of income and employment, so a withdrawal from ski tourism may severely affect the local economy if there aren't any associated plans for economic development or employment creation. • Potential for more environmentally-friendly and less destructive tourism.

APPENDIX 5

Significant natural disasters in the Alps 1980-2005

Date	Region	Event	Deaths	Losses (€ m)** economic	insured
12.7.1984	Southern Germany	Hailstorm		950	480
18.-28.7.1987	Northern Italy (Veltlin)	Landslide, flash floods	44	625	0
July-Aug. 1987	Switzerland (Brig)	Floods	8	800	175
25.2.-1.3.1990	Entire Alps	Winter storms Vivian, Wiebke	7*	700*	460*
Sept.- Oct. 1993	Switzerland (Brig)	Floods	2	620	320
4.-6.11.1994	Northern Italy (Veltlin)	Floods	64	9,300	65
Jan.- March 1999	Entire Alps	Avalanches, winter damages	108	850	150
May 1999	Germany, Switzerland	Floods	8	670	290
3.-7.7.2000	Austria	Hailstorm	2	125	70
14.-21.10.2000	Northern Italy, Switzerland	Landslide, storm surge	38	8,500	420
6.-7.7.2001	Southern Germany	Severe storm	6	300	200
7.-8.7.2001	Northern Italy	Tornado		175	30
3.8.2001	Southern Germany, Bavaria	Severe storm, hailstorm		300	200
August 2002	Southern Germany, Austria Italy	Floods, severe storm, Hailstorm	30	10,000	1,000
2./3.1. 2003	Germany, Switzerland France	Winter storm Calvann, floods	6	305	100
August 2003	Austria, Switzerland, Italy France	Severe storm, landslides	5	500	5
20.-27.8.2005	Schwitzerland, Germany Austria	Floods	11	2,550	1,270

* only Austria and Switzerland

** original values

Source: Munich Re, Geo Risks Research, © 01/2006 **NatCatSERVICE ®**

APPENDIX 6

Prevention policy in the French Alps

A.6. Figure 1. **Evolution of PPRs adoption in France, 1980-2005**

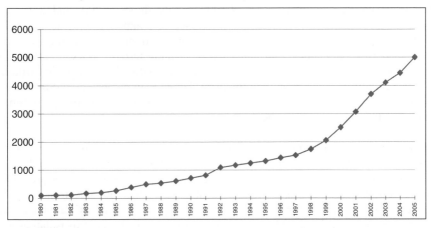

Source: DPPR.

A.6. Figure 2. **Natural hazards in the French Alps: Exposure, events, and prevention plans**

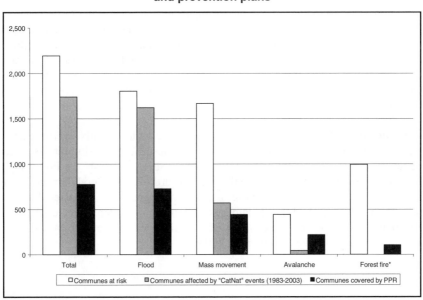

* CatNat insurance does not cover forest fire.
Source: DPPR.

APPENDIX 7

Risk transfer mechanisms in the Alps

Like many other regions in the world, recent extreme events in Alpine areas, such as the avalanches and windstorms of 1999, and the floods of 2002 and 2005, have imposed significant losses to the various insurance or compensation schemes (CCR, 2005; Kamber, 2006; Prettenthaler and Vetters, 2006). Current climate change scenarios suggest increasing frequency and intensity of natural hazards (OcCC, 2003) and increasing insured damages related to these events (SwissRe, 2006). Coupled with the persistence of current socio-economic trends in Alpine regions, which tend to increase exposure to hazards and assets vulnerability, natural hazards are likely to further increase the stress on insurance schemes.

For insurers, increasing probabilities of extreme events and losses can threaten solvency and would require greater capital reserves (see A.7 Figure 1). In general, larger losses due to greater frequency or magnitude of hazards also lead to higher premiums. Reduced insurance coverage and availability may be another possible response. This response would, however, imply large economic and social costs as individuals and local economies would have to bear the financial burden of hazards in isolation with great impact on their economic development.

Recent experience within Alpine risk transfer schemes

In France, extremes events increased financial pressure on the CCR reserves in the last decade. The windstorm and floods of 1999 resulted in large damages and insurance losses across the country, requiring the injection of EUR 450 million directly from the government to honour the stop-loss agreement and the unlimited guarantee. These recent events led to some reforms of the program in 2000. In order to replenish the CCR reserves, the premium surcharge on property insurance went up to 12% (CCR, 2005).

In Austria, outflows from the disaster fund have varied greatly overtime and the reserves of the Disaster Fund have on occasion been insufficient during the last decade, thus requiring direct inflows from the governments (See A.7. Figure 2). Following the 2002 flood, the small number of people that were insured against flood damages led to a large political pressure to compensate hazards damages. The Disaster Fund was insufficient to compensate for all damages and the government injected EUR 500 million in the Fund, out of which EUR 250 million were intended to compensate damages on private properties (Hyll *et al.*, 2003).

A.7. Figure 1. **Potential impact of climate change on loss probability distribution and implications for insurers**

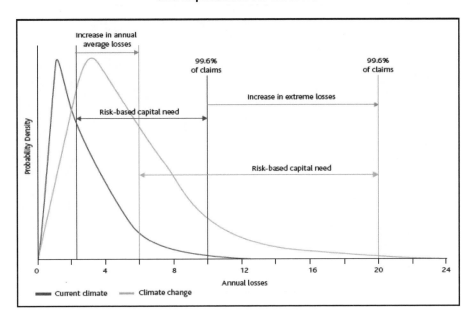

Source: Association of British Insurers (2005).

A.7. Figure 2. **Evolution of CCR's reserves and insured losses**

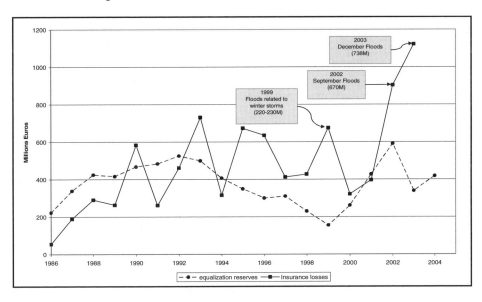

Source: CCR (2005).

A.7. Figure 3. **Compensation outflows from the Austrian Disaster Fund**

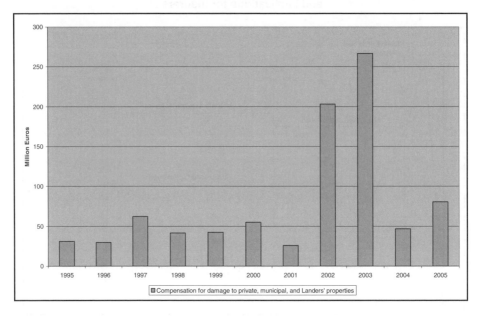

Source: Data from BMF.

In the Swiss cantons covered by CIMs, damages increased over the last decades and extreme losses resulted from the avalanches and winter storms of 1999 as well as the floods of 2005 (see A.7. Figure 4). At the same time, property insurance premiums (including natural hazards coverage) have decreased by more than 30% over the 1981-1999 period. Since 1999 premiums have slightly increased. The low sensitivity of premium to large events and losses may be due to the financial health of CIMs and to their ability to foster prevention through building codes and restrictions. However, it is questionable whether such trend in damages (+8.1%) can be sustainable in the longer term.

Some measures undertaken to respond to increasing damages

In France, private insurers also reacted to the increasing damages linked to natural hazards in creating the *Mission des sociétés d'assurances pour la Connaissance et la Prévention des risques naturels* (MRN) in 2000. The objectives of MRN are to 1) compile knowledge on hazards and facilitate its access to insurers, 2) increase the involvement of insurers in natural hazards prevention measures, 3) diffuse information on natural hazards insurance and linkages with prevention to policyholders.

In Austria, following the 2002 floods, the private insurance sector in partnership with the Federal Ministry of Agriculture, Forestry, Environment and Water Management (BMLFUW) created a flood mapping program called *HORA*. The objective of this program was to provide information to the general public and raise flood risk awareness. The flood mapping realised under HORA also represents a first step in improving the planning of prevention efforts and increases the capacity of private insurers to offer flood insurance coverage. (http://www.hochwasserrisiko.at/)

A.7. Figure 4. **Insured losses due to natural hazards in Switzerland**

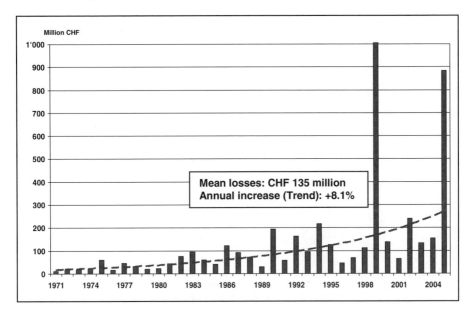

Source: Kamber (2006).

OECD PUBLICATIONS, 2, rue André-Pascal, 75775 PARIS CEDEX 16
PRINTED IN FRANCE
(97 2007 06 1 P) ISBN 92-64-03168-5 – No. 55421 2007